the ironic eye

the ironic eye

ANDREW RIEMER

Angus&Robertson
An imprint of HarperCollins*Publishers*

An Angus & Robertson Publication

Angus&Robertson, an imprint of
HarperCollins*Publishers*
25 Ryde Road, Pymble, Sydney, NSW 2073, Australia
31 View Road, Glenfield, Auckland 10, New Zealand

First published by Angus & Robertson Publishers, Australia, 1994

National Library of Australia
Cataloguing-in-Publication data:
   Riemer, A. P. (Andrew P.).
   The ironic eye: the poetry and prose of Peter Goldsworthy.

   ISBN 0 207 18250 7.

   1. Goldsworthy, Peter, 1951- –Criticism and interpretation.
   I. Title.

A821.3

Cover painting by Dee Jones.
Cover design by Robyn Latimer
Printed in Australia by McPherson's Printing Group, Victoria

9 8 7 6 5 4 3 2 1
97 96 95 94

CONTENTS

ACKNOWLEDGMENTS

HarperCollins Publishers gratefully acknowledge Wakefield Press for permission to reproduce excerpts from *Bleak Rooms* © Peter Goldsworthy 1988, Wakefield Press, Kent Town, South Australia.

PREFACE

An account of how this book came into being and what it hopes to achieve may be of some use. I was asked, early in 1993, whether I would consider writing a short critical study of Peter Goldsworthy's work. My initial hesitation had nothing to do with its quality. At the time I had read much of Goldsworthy's poetry and the two novels, *Maestro* and *Honk If You Are Jesus*, both of which I had reviewed for *The Sydney Morning Herald*. I found his work admirable for its economy, for its intellectual integrity and for its often surprising depth of feeling. My misgivings came from an entirely different source.

Although I had met Goldsworthy only once or twice, and then fleetingly, I did not relish the prospect of writing about a living author. That reluctance may have been the consequence of my having spent most of my working life in a university, where you usually write about authors who are safely dead. Its fundamental cause was, however, more respectable: Goldsworthy is still a relatively young man; admirable though his work is, the best is probably yet to come. The question arose therefore: where does that leave a book-length critical study, no matter how modest in proportions? I recalled the sad plight of an acquaintance whose study of a well-known author appeared a few weeks before the publication of a remarkable work by that author, a work which obliged critics to reconsider the scope and significance of his earlier work. Was it too risky, I asked myself, to embark on this otherwise alluring project?

A meeting with Goldsworthy was arranged. We met over dinner in a bistro, surrounded by the type of people who look as if they might carry portable phones and conduct complicated business deals between (or during) courses. At first the conversation was cautious and desultory—each of us was, I think, slightly apprehensive, perhaps fazed by the not entirely appropriate ambience. We discussed the latest literary gossip, talked about poetry and (obliquely) about Goldsworthy's poetic ambitions. He spoke a little about his latest project, an as yet untitled volume of short fiction which he was thinking of calling *Little Deaths*. Eventually we got on to a topic that occupies considerable space in his fiction and verse: music. Perhaps it was a safe topic, perhaps it represented a genuine point of empathy, but whatever the explanation, by the end of the evening I found myself more than willing to write this short book. It was, accordingly, written during the winter of 1993, and takes Goldsworthy's career as far as *Little Deaths*, which I saw in manuscript, and subsequently in advance printed copies.

What this book hopes to achieve is more difficult to state. It seems to me best to begin by noting certain constraints. I soon came to realise in the early stages of writing that Goldsworthy's fiction would have to occupy the greater space. That ran the risk of making his poetry seem secondary or even possibly irrelevant, something very far from my estimate of its value and significance. As things turned out, the solution to the problem posed by that constraint lay in the nature of Goldsworthy's work. His poetry, I came to understand, considers, in the characteristic way of short lyric verse, many of the issues and preoccupations of his fiction. I found indeed that the material of some of his poems made its way directly into the fiction, as is the case with Mara's recollection of a visit to the Père Lachaise cemetery in Paris in *Honk If You Are Jesus* and the poem 'Cimetière Père Lachaise'. This book could, therefore, begin with a consideration of Goldsworthy's verse, based on his 1990 collection; this could also act as a point of reference for the discussion of his novels and short stories.

Considering the short fiction presented another problem, a different set of constraints. Two of the three volumes published before his first novel, *Maestro*, were (as far as I knew) out of print. It seemed to me necessary to take them into account, nevertheless, because they contain the germs of many of the preoccupations of the novels. A discussion of those volumes of short stories would lead, naturally enough, to *Maestro* and *Honk If You Are Jesus*. Moreover, it seemed inevitable that this book should end with a consideration of the latest of Goldsworthy's publications, *Little Deaths*, especially with a discussion of the substantial novella 'Jesus Wants Me For A Sunbeam', which represents a notable achievement and a remarkable development in Goldsworthy's fiction. For that reason, the final chapter focuses on the novella at the expense of the other stories, which, despite their interest, seem to me not significantly different in ambition and scope from those in the earlier collections of short stories.

There remained one, somewhat dubious, item. In 1992 Goldsworthy and Brian Matthews published *Magpie*, a curious literary spoof or shaggy-dog story. It concerns a certain John Bennett, a character in a novel entitled 'Magpie' by William Barrett, a Professor of English (such as Matthews himself, perhaps). The conceit of this odd collaboration is that John Bennett is split into two largely antithetical individuals—John and Bennett—when an intrusive editor takes it upon himself to 'improve' Barrett's text. *Magpie* contains some amusing incidents as the two halves of John Bennett search for each other in a concentration camp for unrealised or still-born characters. More importantly, it may reveal something of an underlying anxiety in some of Goldsworthy's work—and no doubt that of Matthews as well—about the role of the writer in the modern world. That seemed insufficient warrant, nevertheless, to engage in an extended discussion of a work which must, by its very nature, lie outside Goldsworthy's own *oeuvre*.

Finally, there is the matter of critical approach. This book attempts to preserve, in a more lasting form perhaps, some of the more attractive qualities of literary journalism. In other words, it is not a work of academic scholarship, nor a study guide to Goldsworthy's work, but a discussion of some fine poetry and fiction addressed to the general reader. As is often the case with literary journalism, restriction of space made it impossible for me to discuss published criticism of Goldsworthy's books.

Within the modest scope of this study, I have attempted to achieve critical integrity without recourse to the techniques of academic criticism. I wished to avoid, above all, the often cacophonous jargon in which contemporary academic criticism garbs at times quite commonplace notions. I wanted to allow my individual reading of Goldsworthy's work to provide a focus for a discussion addressed to well-informed, non-specialist readers. How far I have succeeded in the aim of writing serious literary criticism in the language of ordinary discourse is not for me to judge. There is one ambition, however, that I may claim to have achieved: this is a book without footnotes.

Andrew Riemer
Sydney
18 October 1993

Chapter One

The Poet of Small Spaces

In 1991, at the age of forty, Peter Goldsworthy published a small volume of 'Selected Poems 1970—1990' under the whimsical title *This Goes With That*. His author's note shares many of the characteristics of his writing—ironic, poised, amused and displaying an attractive mixture of modesty and confidence:

> To publish a Selected Poems at an age which—to me at least—still feels like the first blush of youth is fortunately not without precedent, and my excuse is better than most: my first two books are both out of print, and my current rule of production is such that a third collection, even a collection as slim as the first two, is many years away. This go-slow is only partly due to the belief that Less is almost always More . . .

Goldsworthy's publications, when compared with those of his more prolific contemporaries, are modest in extent. Apart from those slender volumes of verse, he has published four collections of short stories, *Archipelagoes* (1982), *Zooing* (1986), *Bleak Rooms* (1988) and *Little Deaths* (1993); two novels, *Maestro* (1991) and *Honk If You Are Jesus* (1992) and, in collaboration with Brian Matthews, *Magpie* (1992), a curious literary spoof which reveals, perhaps unwittingly, the anxieties of a writer attempting

3

to come to terms with some theories of literature current in the closing decades of the twentieth century.

This is not, by any definition, a large *oeuvre*. It is nevertheless clear that Goldsworthy has already established for himself an enviable reputation. His name may not fall trippingly from the tongue whenever the Australian literary avant garde is discussed, yet the imaginative coherence and ethical integrity of his work have impressed many readers and critics. It commands respect because of its solid achievement, but also, and just as importantly, because Goldsworthy has managed to contain both his verse and fiction within mostly traditional literary forms and devices—in the public domain, so to speak—without compromising his integrity. He is not a populist, yet his work has little or anything of the arcane about it. He is not uncommitted, yet none of his writing seems to be intent on pushing political or ideological barrows. He occupies a middle ground devoted to certain virtues—moderation among them—which may not be as irresistibly alluring now as they once were. His writing is conservative in the best sense, free of bombast, free of rhetorical flourishes, free of special pleading. And above all, in his prose as much as in his verse, there is a consistent preoccupation with concision, with the avoidance of the redundant or the otiose.

These qualities are reflected, perhaps, in the two sides of his public personality. Goldsworthy is not the first medical practitioner to pursue a writing career—Chekhov inevitably comes to mind. Nor is he alone among contemporary Australian writers in pursuing two careers: lawyers, accountants, dentists, as well as several medical practitioners besides Goldsworthy, are represented in lists of books currently in print. Indeed, it is more than likely that most contemporary writers—elsewhere as much as in Australia—find it impossible to devote themselves fully to their literary preoccupations. Nevertheless it is difficult to avoid the temptation of making a specific connection between the two sides of Goldsworthy's public career.

The neatness and precision of his work, its avoidance of excess and its concern with form would seem to be connected with what one likes to imagine is the scientific temper—at least until David Foster's whirling fantasies come to mind. Most of the poems in *This Goes With That* reveal an elegant neatness; they sit decorously on the page. The inessential has been pared down or honed away in a way reminiscent, perhaps, of the scientist's careful probing, discarding the redundant, eliminating the inaccurate or the inapplicable. The result is, at times, apparently trivial; conciseness begins to seem abrupt, as in the opening poem, entitled 'Razor':

> *Carving this same face*
> *out of soap, each morning*
> *slightly less perfectly.*

Twentieth-century poetry is not unfamiliar with such epigrammatic innocence. Ezra Pound obviously stands behind 'Razor', as does the cult of Chinese poetry at the turn of the century, or the later fashion for haikus. Yet the poem with which Goldsworthy decided to open his selection—a selection that does not follow, he is careful to state, any chronological arrangement—reveals affinities with different, perhaps more robust, possibilities for poetry.

'Razor' is anything but an evocation of evanescent moods, or the deliberate refusal to have any truck with meanings or suggestions implicit in the traditions of symbolist verse from which such miniatures often derive. This, as most of the other pieces in the collection, is a statement, an attempt to convey not merely an experience—even if it should be an experience as mundane as the daily act of shaving—but the implications, both personal and public, of that experience. The poem encompasses time and therefore inevitably decay, as well as a sense of regret—controlled, muted, yet nonetheless strongly suggested.

Goldsworthy's poetry probably has more to do with the traditions of confessional verse, as exemplified in our time by a poet such as Lowell, than with the abstractions which his small and compacted poems seem to imply. Most of the verse in the collection reveals its affinity with the ironic traditions of modernism. The poet—as much as the novelist or short-story writer if it comes to that—is aware of the paradoxical absurdity of most human actions or states. Sometimes, as in 'Act Six', the second poem in the collection, that sense is close to a type of nihilism, yet even in such cases a protesting voice makes itself heard, although only at the last moment:

> *Act six begins*
> *when the curtain falls,*
> *the corpses arise,*
> *the daggers are cleaned.*

> *Act six*
> *places Juliet in the supermarket,*
> *Mr Macbeth on the 8.15.*

> *In act six*
> *Hamlet sucks a tranquilliser,*

> *Romeo washes up*
> *and death*
> *is gentle and anonymous:*
> *Lear's life-support*
> *switched discreetly off.*

Sophisticated irony, the insistence on the ordinariness of life, a world of supermarkets and tranquillisers rather than the spectacular finality of tragedy, is converted into something close to anguish: death should not be gentle and anonymous—it would be better, perhaps, to die like the old Lear, raging against a meaningless universe. That note will be heard again, in 'Jesus Wants Me For A Sunbeam', the chilling novella that brings *Little Deaths* to a climax.

For such a sensibility anger and passion may be expressed only by oblique means. King Lear may howl against men of stone; the ironist, by contrast, may only suggest or imply. This attitude is not so much the product of rationalism or of a refusal to admit to the possibility of those things which cannot be verified by inquiry, as a product of scepticism, the corollary, one might argue, of the scientific temper. That scepticism comes to be explored and rigorously tested in *Honk If You Are Jesus*, where the rational and the miraculous are placed in often hilarious conjunction. In Goldsworthy's verse the longing for something that lies beyond the coolly rational receives at times quite explicit articulation, as in 'Give Me Some Kind Of Sign':

> *I want the unambiguous reassurance*
> *of terror. I want to wake*
> *at night screaming, tonight.*

Haunt me, spooks, flicker
my reading-lamp, repossess
my house, give me some kind

of hard evidence.
I feel so chill and lonely
without you.

❦

The poems in *This Goes With That* explore, therefore, the modernist predicament, which is also, of course, the predicament of the modern world. We are not haunted by spooks and phantoms unless we are unfortunate (or fortunate) enough to have experienced the horrors of our century in the way that Eduard Keller, the maestro of *Maestro*, experienced at first hand the madness of the time. Our world is not particularly adept at offering either hope or despair. The site the modern sensibility occupies most comfortably is that ironic scepticism which distinguishes most of Goldsworthy's writing. Such a state of mind may lead, at times, to a refusal to recognise value anywhere. Or else it may explore, define and accurately chart the predicament itself, in a manner not unlike the way in which a diagnosis of an illness might be achieved—except that Goldsworthy the poet cannot (and indeed should not) offer cures or nostrums. To define the state or predicament is often sufficient:

Church bells ring in the far blue, gently
itching, but these Sunday mornings
we believe in nothing, not even in Love . . .
('After the Ball')

At times, in some of the lesser pieces in the collection, Goldsworthy is content merely with recording or defining, embellishing his data, as it were, with sophistication and whimsy, yet conveying little apart from sophistication itself. 'Bees', the last of a sequence entitled 'A Small Bestiary', illustrates the elegant triviality which threatens this kind of verse:

> *Bees*
> *have small furry pelts*
> *hard to keep from getting sticky.*
>
> *Their languages*
> *are dance and telepathy.*
>
> *Inside each bee*
> *is delicate machinery*
> *a noisy watch mechanism.*
>
> *Some kamikaze freely for the Empress.*
> *Others, at the end, look back with pride*
> *on an 8 oz jar in the supermarket.*

However, the majority of the poems in *This Goes With That* fill their small spaces, those tidily, one might say scientifically, contrived containers, with greater ambiguity, and with at least a longing for passion and for fury of the kind which may only be hinted at in such cleanly scrubbed structures.

One potent way of achieving those textures is provided by music, Goldsworthy's preoccupation, solace or perhaps obsession. In both of his novels, and especially in *Maestro*, music and its cultural—perhaps even spiritual—implications offer paradigms for experiences not readily to hand in the commonplace worlds charted in those books: a dreary pre-Tracy Darwin in *Maestro*, the glitz and glitter of the Gold Coast in *Honk If You Are Jesus*. Music flits through the collections of short stories and several of the more impressive poems in *This Goes With That*.

'Gustav Mahler: Songs on the Death of Children' provides the clearest instance of the manner in which Goldsworthy's imagination draws resonance and complexity from music, that is to say from that high culture from which Juliet in the supermarket and Mr Macbeth on the 8.15 have also emerged. The title refers to Mahler's *Kindertotenlieder* (*Songs on the Death of Children*) a lushly romantic, agonised song cycle for voice and orchestra composed in 1903 that was prompted by the death of Mahler's young daughter.

The poem confines an experience of some complexity within the small space of a form that bears a passing resemblance to a sonnet:

> *It's snowing in Adelaide*
> *on the gramophone,*
> *white hiss and static at 78 rpm:*
> *snowing in Vienna, in Adelaide.*
>
> *It's snowing on a father's grief,*
> *on a tear-smudged manuscript,*
> *on a garret on Freudstrasse:*
> *it's snowing on the soundtrack of your life.*
>
> *It's snowing in Vienna, in Adelaide*
> *until I lift the needle off,*
> *and then it's fine and clear,*
>
> *and your music walks away,*
> *on snowshoes of soft violins,*
> *into the silence of the air.*

Several of the poems based on musical concerns in *This Goes With That* achieve greater poise or a finer imaginative integration of their themes than this. There may indeed be a sense of strain in 'Gustav Mahler: Songs on the Death of Children', revealed by the less than happy contrivance of 'it's snowing on the soundtrack of your life', or even perhaps in the phrase 'on snowshoes of soft violins'. For all that, and possibly as a result of its relative lack of poise or confidence, this 'displaced' sonnet, with its obvious use of a quasi-musical recurring motif, illuminates the assumptions, preoccupations or principles that stand behind much of Goldsworthy's work; the title itself may indeed have been the germ from which the splendid novella in *Little Deaths* grew.

'Gustav Mahler: Songs on the Death of Children', or the much more oblique 'Richard Strauss: A Hero's Life'—'music a weightless ocean/ spills like piss from your skull'—or even the more lighthearted 'Piano Stool'—'Frederic coughs, Old Bach snores/Wolf lies down with Franz'—implicitly assume an easy familiarity with those monuments of high culture that formed the often unquestioned standards of the world into which Goldsworthy was born, and to which he seems, moreover, to have remained dedicated. That familiarity, which recognises the pertinence of the musical transformation of Mahler's grief in an Adelaide far distant from Vienna, an Adelaide where it snows only metaphorically as the needle ploughs the shellac grooves, or the familiarity that alludes to the affinity between Schubert and Hugo Wolf, the great masters of lieder, represents a set of cultural standards, and beyond them a system of secular belief, that Goldsworthy, along with people of his background, used to accept almost without question.

Goldsworthy, the biographical details printed in his books tell us, was born in 1951 in Minalton in South Australia, grew up in various country towns and finished his schooling in Darwin. A sequence of poems entitled 'Autobiograffiti' conveys a sharply etched sense of the moral and cultural horizons of the world that nurtured him. It was an Australia which, at the time of his birth, was beginning to experience the pressures that would change it, within the next thirty or forty years, almost beyond recognition. It was, in a sense, an uncomplicated world. He was born:

> *in a small town*
> *with a large graveyard.*
>
> *There were four pubs*
> *but five churches.*

It was also a world of certainties and rituals where:

> *parcels arrived from the Country*
> *Lending Library in the city.*
>
> *There was a wall of china*
> *on the dresser . . .*
>
> *to use any other description*
> *would be perverse.*

Memories of that world provide a basis for much of Goldsworthy's work, whether in the precise and confined spaces of his poems or in his explorations of later, perhaps less innocent decades in his stories and novels. His stance is, as always, ironic—an essentially urban sophistication looks back at a way of life that proved at length incapable of withstanding the pressures of more complex and perhaps more exhilarating times. That sophistication recognises the limitations of such existence. Yet it also registers its capacity, in individuals if not in society as a whole, to learn, in that world of simplicities, the fundamental ambiguity of life:

> *Between yes and no*
> *there are some things,*
>
> *my mother taught*
> *in many ways.*
>
> *Between the lines*
> *(she sang) is space,*
>
> *between the colours*
> *black and white,*
>
> *those other colours,*
> *there.*

Such knowledge counterbalances the other, constricting knowledge which was an inevitable component of that world:

> *At school*
> *I believed everything*
> *I was told . . .*

From that world he travelled, physically and spiritually, to the 'bitumen estuary' driven by:

> *Something less definite*
> *than ambition . . .*
>
> *Here were smart cosmetics:*
> *knowledge, thickly applied,*

> *and sophistication,*
> *a ratchet winding*
> *one direction only,*
>
> *even more tightly.*

The tension that arises as those two worlds meet (and from the knowledge that there is always something between yes and no) produce a conviction—or a longing, for the two are not entirely inimical—affirming the individual's duty to strive for integrity, a search which provides the preoccupation for much of Goldsworthy's writing.

> *As for the claim that Perfection*
> *recedes infinitesimally*
> *with each incremental step closer:*
>
> *enough. I have never believed in algebra,*
> *its untouchable verbs. I have seen tricks*
> *on blackboards, yet gone home knowing*
>
> *that even parallel lines touch*
> *eventually, for theirs is the kingdom*
> *of the real, free from definition . . .*

And that conviction, or longing, emerges, finally and paradoxically, from the certainties and simplicities of that narrow world where every question has an answer:

> *What Did You Get For Mental?*
> *my father sternly asked each night.*
> *Ten, I said, and seldom lied.*

The stories and novels provide more substantial images of that world, of its certainties and its hypocrisies as well. It may have been smugly self-satisfied in its conviction of its own values, yet it did place value, too, on possibilities of transcendence, so to speak, which gave it some strength and viability. It respected what we may call, imprecisely and often pompously, culture, by way of the parcels of books from the Country Lending Library, or the Gilbert and Sullivan evenings to which the narrator's parents are devoted in several short stories and in *Maestro*. That permitted a broadening of intellectual and moral horizons—a contact with other possibilities of life, whether through the snowstorm of a revolving shellac disc transmitting the sounds of *Kindertotenlieder*, or the expectation that one would, as a matter of course, get ten out of ten for mentals or rise to the demands of Czerny.

Goldsworthy's work moves within the spaces provided by such a tension, to chart, with the precision and lack of excess for which his verse is notable, the certainties and anxieties of a life that has left behind the world of four pubs and five churches, to wander, physically and spiritually, among the famous dead at the 'Cimetière Père Lachaise':

> *these days I prefer Chopin*
> *his grave is over there. As for seasonal beliefs*
> *I have no faith in resurrection, or in anything else right now*
> *except the need for tidiness. I rise and bin my bottle,*
> *and walk away clutching my map of the dead*
> *and my single long-stem rose, bypassing Gertrude and Oscar,*
> *searching somewhere between Chopin's grave*
> *and Proust's, for the Tomb of the Homesick Tourist,*
> *open-doored, perhaps, as if ready to receive.*

It returns, though not without misgivings, to that other world, far from Chopin's grave, or from Oscar's or

Gertrude's, to the place where tidiness seems of paramount importance, as 'Credo' makes clear:

> *I believe in the infinite line,*
> *the straight line between points*
> *and the equality of all right angles.*
> *Amen.*

The celebration of these virtues is not without anxiety, however:

> *I like to keep things*
> *inside things. I like to keep*
> *adequate records.*
> *I like to gazette.*

Finally the anxiety is dominant, and introduces a note of some harshness and brutality:

> *I like collecting things*
> *and looking up their names in books.*
> *I like Killing Jars.*
>
> *Always I will prefer the unblemished butterfly*
> *pinned to a mounting board*
> *in the hard cone of a 60-watt desk-lamp*
> *to the tattered joy*
> *circling in a column of dusty sunlight*
> *somewhere.*

The neat, tidy spaces of Goldsworthy's poems, sitting primly on the white pages of *This Goes With That*, contain these tensions and ambiguities within a restrained lyric grace. His verse is modest, finely crafted and decorous. It is neither bold nor adventurous, but it avoids blandness and complacency through its ability to place itself in relation to experiences and possibilities of life (or of death) that are anything but bland or complacent. That might well be a vicarious way of going about things, an attempt at density of texture by contagion so to speak. Cultural monuments—Shakespeare and Mahler, the famous dead buried in Paris—may be markers for what Goldsworthy cannot allow himself to articulate. Passion and fury are absent from his verse, or if they make their presence felt, it is there by virtue of a muted irony.

His fiction, as much as his verse, displays such reining-in, such reluctance to give head to passions that he seems able only to approach obliquely. There is generally a sense of anxiety throughout Goldsworthy's work that he might lose control, that the neat containers of his poems and tales might be strained by a preference for darkness, by tendencies leading to dangerously uncharted waters. So far, only *Maestro* among his novels and 'Jesus Wants Me For A Sunbeam' in *Little Deaths* have been capable of achieving an accommodation of those menacing presences within the controlled certainties of the world of four pubs and five churches. In his verse, especially in 'After the Ball', which brings *This Goes With That* to a close, the limitation and the anxiety are both eloquently recognised:

> *Late-risen, we sit near breakfast*
> *reading large, simple sentences . . .*
> Compensation Shock, *you read aloud.*
> How can money bring back our son—
> we expected twice as much.

Irony is a defence of sorts, yet powerless before anxieties and suffering, such as the suffering, for instance, that generated and is conveyed by Mahler in *Kindertotenlieder*:

> *You avert your gaze, suddenly giddy,*
> *trying to fix on more distant points.*
> *Music helps: a proper soundtrack*
> *can ennoble the cheapest movie . . .*

The urge is nevertheless to recoil:

> *The only certainty, we joke, are jokes:*
> *one day we* will *be seen dead in church.*
> *And if jokes also are a form of headline,*
> *what matter? Where is the sin*
> *in wanting to read no further,*
> *in refusing to wonder what thinking is like*
> *before we begin to talk about it,*
> *or what a feeling—any feeling—might mean*
> *the last instant before it simples into words?*

In that recoil reside some of the most notable achievements, and also the limitations, of the writer who, at the age of forty, took the not unprecedented step of publishing a volume of selected poems.

Chapter Two

Mapping the Suburbs

Goldsworthy's is an essentially poetic sensibility. The small-scale, precise observations of his poems, their careful adjustments of tone, nuance and implication, and his investment in the poignancy of the moment, of fleeting things, are, on the whole, inimical to the demands of narrative. His emergence as a prose writer of considerable accomplishment was achieved by means of a series of short stories in which the difficult transition from anecdote to narrative seems to have been accomplished by means of careful adjustments, small experiments, until, by the time of his first extended narrative structure, *Maestro*, he had learnt a craft which he could exploit with masterful confidence.

The opening section of *Archipelagoes*, Goldsworthy's first collection of short stories, contains six anecdotal vignettes where the fashioner of prose fictions may be seen emerging from the poet. Each is brief—no more than six pages, three and half in some cases. They are sketches, rather than articulated narrative structures. Where a structure of cause and effect, intrinsic to any notion of narrative, no matter how displaced, is in evidence, the construction remains essentially anecdotal, a juxtaposition of images and incidents, rather than an unravelling or evolution.

These sketches, as is the case with the remainder of the stories in *Archipelagoes*, or those in Goldsworthy's later collections, chart the banality of suburban life. It has been said often enough that Australian life, whether in one of the large cities or in a country town, is essentially suburban, that the totems and icons of Australian society are almost identical throughout the continent. 'Historical Necessity and the Garden Sprinkler', the opening sketch of *Archipelagoes*, locates itself firmly in one of the great preoccupations of Australian culture: the handyman forever struggling with decay, corrosion and drought as he keeps his house in tip-top shape and his grass abundantly watered. Evan's culture hero is Lance Hill, inventor of the Hill's Hoist:

> *just an average sort of bloke—a home handyman who was fed up with his washing dragging in the mud. One morning he whipped up the world's first rotary clothes hoist, and by the end of the day had orders pouring in from all over Adelaide. By the end of the year it was a million-dollar business.*
> *(p. 10)*

There is almost no substance to this anecdote. Evan makes two attempts to rig up a complicated watering system for the narrator's garden. Both fail dismally, but Evan, undaunted, dreams of even greater feats of technological virtuosity, while the narrator comments 'I picked up my watering can, and filled it at the tap' (p. 12).

'Historical Necessity and the Garden Sprinkler' appropriates the techniques and concerns of Goldsworthy's poetry for the purposes of a prose sketch or anecdote. This story, just as most of the stories in *Archipelagoes*, especially those in the opening section, conveys ironic images of the petty fantasies of suburban life. Evan worships technological advance and the home-spun ingenuity of the Lance Hills of this world. Fame and fortune are to be sought not in the grandiose or the elaborate, but in the essentially mundane—the bright idea of the rotary hoist that introduced a revolution into the business of getting the washing dry. Goldsworthy's manipulation of tone and nuance reveals the emptiness, or at least the meanness, of such suburban aspirations. Here is a dreary world devoted to the practical without ever considering whether the worship of ingenuity could, perhaps, be devoted to better ends.

The wry condemnation of Evan's pedestrian ambition is not stated, except by way of a snatch or two of dialogue. Rather, it is conveyed in the manner in which poetry, especially of the kind Goldsworthy practises, will focus upon images and objects that encapsulate often quite complex social, ethical or even spiritual preoccupations. Such an essentially imagistic disposition finds it difficult to flower into the necessary condition of fiction, a concern with people and their relationships disclosed within the flux of time.

Of the stories in the opening section of *Archipelagoes*, only 'La Haute Cuisine Australienne' manages to rise above the anecdotal towards some sort of fictional complexity. The opening sentence annunciates both the story's preoccupations and its structural conceit, as though this were a musical composition:

Kate had been working on the Great Australian Dish for years,

> *but wasn't any closer to realising her ambition than she had*
> *been at the age of thirteen when she dunked her first lamington*
> *in coconut and melted chocolate.*
> *(p. 27)*

Nor does she achieve her ambition. At the end of the story, having opened a restaurant purveying what she imagines to be an indigenous version of *nouvelle cuisine*, and having abandoned it in favour of other attempts, notably at serving Aboriginal food—and replacing the prints and artefacts on the walls each time—she fulfils her true potential, as the narrator finds when he returns to her restaurant after a period of absence:

> *I didn't recognise the restaurant at first—she'd knocked*
> *archways through the dividing walls and extended along the*
> *entire block of shops. And there was a queue outside fifty*
> *metres long . . .*
>
> *In the backroom behind her, I could see Kate sitting at a table*
> *piled high with cubes of sponge. I watched as she methodically*
> *dipped them in a bowl of melted chocolate, rolled them in a*
> *bowl of grated coconut.*
> *(p. 32)*

The construction and the ambitions of this story are identical to those of the shorter anecdotal pieces, such as the sketch concerning the backyard handyman's attempts to emulate the singular success of Lance Hill. Kate's flirtation with what she sees as the emblems of cosmopolitan sophistication, derived no doubt from the glossy images of glycerine-covered dishes in cooking books, reveals the naivety of Australia's infatuation with the exotic and the cosmopolitan. Her attempts to evolve an Australian *haute cuisine* without any particular aptitude for the task, or without the necessary skill or training, speak of the banality of suburban ambitions. The manner in which she adopts fashionable catchcries, whether those connected with cosmopolitan sophistication or non-racist attitudes (in her Aboriginal food phase), renders her 'an earnest bore'—though the narrator recognises himself as 'a flippant smartarse'. When she reverts to the one skill she possesses, a skill learnt in that country town from which she fled to experience the delights and challenges of the metropolis, she confirms the fundamentally suburban horizons of a world where the lamington is king.

Nevertheless, the story has a somewhat denser texture than the anecdote about the garden sprinkler or the other slighter pieces in *Archipelagoes*. It hints at relationships, and at small, insignificant clashes of personality. The narrator of 'Historical Necessity and the Garden Sprinkler' is mostly a cipher, trundled on stage so that he might enact, at the end of the story, the implicit commentary on Evan's ambitions. In 'La Haute Cuisine Australienne', by contrast, the narrator displays a certain insensitivity when—perhaps justifiably—he mocks Kate's attempts to evolve a cuisine based on indigenous food:

I thought a little joke might break the ice, and cheer her up.
'What about a drink?' I said. 'Where's the metho list?'
  It didn't break the ice—but it certainly broke something.
  'What a filthy thing to say!' she exploded. 'It's not even
funny—it's sick!'
  She stood up, whisked my half-eaten fish from under my
nose, and walked out.
  'We don't serve racists in this establishment! Nyuntu ma
kumpurawa—*that's Pitjantjatjara for piss off, whitefeller!'*
(p. 31)

That little drama is authentic fiction, it contains a series of innuendos, implications about both of the characters that cannot easily be conveyed in the type of lyrical verse Goldsworthy favours. It represents, moreover, a method, a structural and narrative disposition, that is elaborated in his more complex stories and in the novels.

Such characteristics are fleetingly evident in the pages of *Archipelagoes*; most of the stories in the collection remain anecdotal, providing restricted scope for effects which came to be exploited more consistently in Goldsworthy's second collection, *Zooing*. Nevertheless, the earlier volume already contains the chief preoccupations of Goldsworthy's later and more adventurous work. It maps the territory the later stories and novels explore, one charted in different ways in his verse—the fundamentally suburban horizons of the post-war Australian middle classes.

It is a restricted world, one largely immune to suffering, resistant to the heroic, the visionary or the possessed. It is mostly a comfortable world, the conflicts of which are likely to be mildly ideological, as in 'Memoirs of a small "m" Marxist'—a sketch concerned with a brief affair between two students, one, the boy, an easy-going hedonist, the other caught in the trammels of political theory. Or else the stories disclose the way in which marriages can be soured by routine and familiarity, or they explore ironies of the kind contained in the closing story 'Garibaldi Business Machines—the Early Years' where a dedicated materialist beats the narrator, something of a woolly aesthete, at his own game by publishing a highly-regarded novel. This is not, therefore, an adventurous world. The ironically pompous titles of these stories declare that its dreams and disasters are only relatively earth-shaking, and that they are to be contained within the protective cocoon of middle-class life.

Once or twice, nevertheless, Goldsworthy breaks beyond those confines to explore, somewhat tentatively it is true, more disturbing potentialities within such unremarkable people and their lives. 'Cranky Feller', one of the two stories in the collection concerned with black people, deals with the plight of a young Aborigine who tries his luck as a boxer after one of his periodic stints in gaol. 'The People versus Jehova God', in which a group of adolescents test and destroy the faith of their Lutheran pastor, addresses itself to the problems of faith in a secularised world that will recur with greater complexity and hilarity in *Honk if You Are Jesus* and in the novella in *Little Deaths*. In two stories Goldsworthy tries his hand at pastiche—in a tale set in Darwin dealing with the persecution of a Timorese immigrant, and in the curious 'Chapter from a Fictional Science Fiction' depicting a world where your life expectancy relies absolutely on the health of your bank balance.

The most interesting of these stories, however, is a disturbing monologue entitled 'The Misogynist' which explores a more menacing world than most of Goldsworthy's later work. The technique of this fine story is closer to Goldsworthy's verse than to the largely anecdotal procedures of most of the other stories in the collection. It is not constructed around a revealing incident, or at best succession of incidents; rather, the narrator's seemingly random reminiscences of a failed and miserable life weave together a series of apparently disconnected strands that nevertheless come together to disclose, by means of powerfully dark irony, a disturbing vision of a prevalent predicament of modern Australian life.

The narrator is a football coach. Even after he has grown

too old to play, his infatuation with the game continues:

> *So I was always down at the Club—coaching the junior sides,*
> *or running for the seniors. It was a cubbyhole to crawl into*
> *after work, a refuge from the rest of the world. From mortgages,*
> *car payments—all the daily ounces of flesh. And above all,*
> *from the wreckage of my marriage.*
> *(p. 40)*

He takes under his wing a boy, a promising player, whom he hopes to save, by means of football, from what *he* at least sees as the misery of the boy's life:

> *On the way home, I'd drop him off quickly—before his mother*
> *had time to waddle out. I couldn't stand her—one of those loud*
> *fat women with moustaches, who look as though someone has*
> *taken them by an orifice and blown too hard. Her head a red*
> *balloon, her hands inflated gloves, and always shrieking over*
> *the heads of half a dozen grubby brats.*
> *(p. 41)*

The end is predictable. The boy grows up, marries, suffers an injury on the field which brings his career to an end— even though the narrator, who had pushed him to the point of over-exertion, makes him cling, at the end of the story, to his illusions:

> *I couldn't tell him—and even if I could have, he probably*
> *wouldn't have heard. He needed illusions, not truth.*
> * 'Who knows?' I lied to him, as he limped out of football.*
> *'Maybe next season . . .?'*
> *(p. 44)*

More tellingly than the other stories in *Archipelagoes*, 'The Misogynist' reveals the dark implications of Goldsworthy's irony. The petty conflicts and clashes of will or of opinion elsewhere in the volume identify the absurdity of the suburban world they chart. Here, at least by implication, Goldsworthy conveys a sense of betrayal—his portrait of that allegedly archetypal Australian male, the football-worshipping philistine, is informed by a certain menace and anger.

That is a familiar enough stance among recent writers. The worship of the physical, symbolised by the mindless immersion in sport, and the spiritual emptiness of such dedication, have been commonplace in writing about Australian life since at least as early as Lawrence's observations in several episodes of *Kangaroo*. Goldsworthy's story seems, therefore, to align itself with the predominant traditions of modern Australian writing, where writers generally set themselves apart from the philistine materialism of a world of suburban priorities, a world they regard as almost wholly lacking in imagination. Characteristically, that condition or predicament is seen here in terms of the difference between men and women:

I'd met my wife in the staffroom of my first school. She was teaching Art and I was teaching Phys. Ed.— so maybe we didn't have a chance from the start. With no children to glue us together, we just drifted apart. Slowly came unstuck. And her attitude to football didn't help—she was always on my back about it.

'A grown man!' she used to laugh. 'Chasing little balls around a paddock all weekend! What kind of life is that? What kind of meaning?'
(p. 40)

Yet the story is not content to leave it merely at that familiar, ideologically conventional conclusion. The texture of 'The Misogynist', more dense and substantial than elsewhere in *Archipelagoes*, reveals an anxiety, or at least an ambivalence. May nothing be said in favour of a world where the highest aspirations are to chase a little ball around a paddock all weekend? The orthodoxies of a large section of the world in which Goldsworthy grew up, a world reflected in a number of stories in this collection, would insist that there is not. 'The Misogynist', by transmitting these images of a restricted and un-imaginative way of life through a plausible voice, slides into possibilities of celebration. Perhaps there is, after all, some value here, despite the insensitivity, the betrayal, the self-indulgence. There may be, the story implies, some potential for transcendence, even in a world as apparently lacking in imagination as the narrator's:

> *Every time I slip on my tracksuit, I slip back into those memories. The absolute belief in my own muscle, my own ability. A high that was almost religious—in which anything was suddenly possible.*
> (p. 43)

Such transcendence is no doubt risible, petty heroism. Yet this fine story explores possibilities which are markedly contrary to the prevailing tenor of contemporary Australian writing. In a limited and always sceptical manner, Goldsworthy seems to embark on a tentative celebration of the values of the suburban world the stories in *Archipelagoes* explore with such irony. The tension between irony and celebration, and also the anxiety implicit in the connection, form the basis of some of the more memorable pieces in his next collection, *Zooing*, as well as in his later, more complex stories and novels.

❧

The suburban world charted in *Archipelagoes* is explored somewhat more adventurously in Goldsworthy's second collection of stories. Several are longer, more intricate structures than the essentially anecdotal contents of the earlier collection. One or two of these return to the themes and devices of earlier stories in a more complex manner.

'The Law and Procedure of Meetings in Australia and New Zealand, and I' continues the concern evident in several of the stories in the earlier collection with the ideological preoccupations of the urban middle classes, more particularly where lightly worn political allegiances come into conflict with the characters' personalities, and their social and sexual rivalries. The ponderous title indicates the affinity between this story, dealing with two couples who had shared a house in the early years of their relationships, and a story such as 'La Haute Cuisine Australienne'. The emphasis is also much the same— ironic disillusionment when the narrator, who has followed successfully a lucrative career which has nevertheless left his childless marriage in tatters, finds that he envies the messy, indigent life of the other couple, who are always broke, always preoccupied by their brood of children, yet somehow living a fuller, richer life than his:

I still picture them from time to time—at nights, mostly, when I can't sleep. I see them clearly in my mind's eye: rolling down their narrow mountain road each morning, crawling back up that same road each night—the children crammed into the back

31

> *. . . I see them toiling away, day in, day out—bound together*
> *till death do them part, I suppose, by all their schedules and*
> *agendas, stuck fast by all the nappy solutions, the milk*
> *formulas and baby shit, indissoluble glue.*
>   *Poor bastards, I tell myself. Poor, lucky, lucky bastards.*
> *(p. 23)*

This story, as with several of the stories in *Zooing*, lays claim to that ground of humanistic values which have provided a persistent preoccupation for writers since the end of the eighteenth century. Goldsworthy's narrator is brought to an understanding similar to that achieved by the spiritual and ethical journeys of Dickens's or George Eliot's characters. The values of worldly success corrupt, or else they are arid. Happiness, or at least whatever degree of contentment may be achieved, resides in human relationships, in love which may flourish—perhaps is only capable of flourishing—in adversity, amid difficult and trying circumstances. Goldsworthy asserts these values by bringing his narrator to an understanding of them in the last line of the story, a tiny epiphany that encapsulates the experience and the implications of his account of two antithetical types of relationships.

To reach back towards the sustaining values of earlier writers is one thing. To articulate them in a very different ethical and political context is another. The late twentieth century does not find such values entirely congenial. They have been too debased, too often sentimentalised, and, it might also be argued, used too often as propaganda to give brutality a smiling face, for them to remain innocent. Goldsworthy's story reveals a recognition of these issues in the way he marshals material which allows him to avoid the potential sentimentality of his narrator's discovery.

One device for avoiding sentimentality is, of course, the cumbersome title. A more telling instance, though, is a conceit that came to be used in much more complex ways in *Maestro*. In the opening sections Paula and Bernie, whom the narrator comes to envy by the end of the story, emerge as bossy prigs. They attempt to direct the management of the shared house in a legalistic, petti-fogging way. Everything has to be done by agreement; agreements have to be achieved by properly constituted meetings conducted in accordance with the procedures laid down in P. E. Joske's *The Law and Procedure of Meetings in Australia and New Zealand*. Yet for all their nitpicking insistence on proper procedures, Bernie and Paula seem only too prepared to exploit a system of their own making, especially whenever they experience one of their 'accidents', the birth of yet another unplanned child.

It is from that perspective that Goldsworthy attempts to bring his readers—by way of his narrator's change of attitude—to a recognition of the fundamentally com-mendable values and possibilities of life inherent in such apparent selfishness and exploitation. The literary procedure may be likened to turning tables, in order to ensure that the 'upbeat' ending does not decline into the cloying and the sentimental.

The device works well enough, but it is limited in its possibilities, or else it requires a longer structure to avoid the type of predictable unpredictability that often haunts such attempts at short fiction. The more memorable stories in *Zooing*, while not contradicting the ethical and social values that become explicit by the end of 'The Law and Procedure of Meetings in Australia and New Zealand, and I', find ways of allowing such values or preoccupations to emerge more by implication or demonstration. In those stories one may observe Goldsworthy's attempts to quell some of the perplexities that writers of fiction who work within broad humanist traditions inevitably encounter in the last decades of an ironic century.

'The Unpleasantness at the Returned Military Officers' Club'—its title a wry glance at Dorothy Sayers, perhaps— is a turning point in the evolution of Goldsworthy from a fashioner of anecdotal prose pieces to the confident novelist. This story is distinguished by the interaction of groups of contrasted characters, each illuminating one aspect of the social world the story explores. The narrative voice is no longer an overarching presence, as it is in some of the stories, or an emerging conscience or consciousness, as it is in others, but an element in a complex design where attitudes and preoccupations clash, or slide over each other, contriving, at length, to produce a much more intricate and substantial disclosure than previously encountered in Goldsworthy's short fiction.

The setting, the characters and the situation are entirely banal, as befits the aspirations of an ironist. A family gathers in a stuffy, somewhat run-down club for returned officers for a sixtieth birthday celebration. Though the place has fallen on hard times—

> *club membership was in decline, and the Committee was*
> *growing increasingly desperate. There had not, after all, been a*
> *war of credible proportions—a war you could get your teeth*
> *into—for years.*
> (p. 41)

—it insists on maintaining standards of dress, cuisine and conduct long abandoned by the world outside. The story begins with a fracas when the narrator and his brother are almost denied entry by a superciliously deferential door-man because of their failure to wear ties.

The mood of mocking comedy continues as the brothers grapple with the ties thoughtfully provided by their father—those unwelcome insignia of a way of life which they had deliberately turned their backs on:

The three of us spent some time trying to apply those
regimental tourniquets. The main problem being, in fact,
exactly that: we were trying. Trying a little too hard, trying to
remember each step in the knotting procedure individually,
instead of just letting our hands do the work.
(p. 45)

Goldsworthy introduces an unexpected element into the texture of this ironic examination of the absurdity of social rituals, where the refusal to wear a tie is as much a striking of attitudes as the absolute insistence that ties must be worn. Having successfully done battle with their ties, the brothers join the family party to find their father in full flight on his favourite topic:

The Russians were on the move, we arrived to hear him
assuring Cassie. And Mum. And anyone else within earshot
willing to listen. The Russians were ready to go at a moment's
notice. At the drop of a magnesium flare. The evidence was
plain to see . . .
(p. 46)

What follows, though, renders this commonplace situation unusual. 'Dad', the seemingly stereotyped 'cold-war warrior' proves to have an unpredictable regard for the Russians; his visit to Moscow, recorded for all time on endless rolls of film, seems to have been the occasion for a curious conversion:

I was never quite sure if he had loved the place, or loathed it,
and I think he was equally confused himself. The Reds had been
the bad guys all his life—until now. Now he had seen their
System with his own two eyes—with his own three eyes,
including his Instamatic—and had seen that it worked. All the
virtues we seemed to have lost, they seemed to have found:
discipline, self-sacrifice, loyalty to commissar and country. In
short, perfect Law and Order.
(p. 48)

The birthday celebration ends in disaster and
embarrassment. The tension between the generations that
rises in the dining-room of the Returned Military Officers'
Club provokes a bizarre 'unpleasantness'. When the
narrator's brother begins making provocative remarks
about excessive consumption in a starving world, 'Dad'
calls his son's bluff and orders bread and dripping to be
produced in place of the customary festive fare. The
consequences are perhaps unexpected: it is 'Dad', the
upholder of law and order, who is summoned by the
committee for 'a quiet word' precisely because he
provoked a fuss in making one of the younger generation
eat his words, so to speak, but also because of his loud
admiration for the despised 'Reds'. The last word is left
with his wife:

'Why did you have to goad him on?' she accused us. 'He's been
in enough trouble at the club as it is, with all his talk about the
Russians . . .'
   We munched our spotted dick and sipped our port in silence
for the rest of the evening. But I couldn't help thinking—if the
Committee blackballed dear old Dad, where would that leave
my own application for membership?
(p. 52)

This is the most developed of the stories in *Zooing*. Others, it is true, explore more disturbing aspects of the suburban world. 'The Blooding' is an account of the narrator's father, a dedicated sportsman, and his callous cruelty to the greyhounds he attempts to raise, and also his cruelty concerning his son's love for those hapless animals. The story is much more savage in its condemnation of the dark aspects of suburbia than the domestic comedy played out in the dining-room of a down-at-heel club. 'Sweet and Sour Story', concerned with the accident-prone Willy Owens, who is nevertheless protected by some curious providence until he is killed one night in a senseless attack, explores with greater force those questions of individual responsibility which form the core of several of these stories. This is also true of 'A Cobbler's Child', a story about alternative, and possibly fraudulent, medicine. Yet 'The Unpleasantness at the Returned Military Officers' Club' points most surely to the novels that were to follow Goldsworthy's volumes of short fiction.

In the context of a banal fuss amidst the stuffy proprieties of that club, Goldsworthy discovers a way of revealing the complexity of attitudes and motives that drive seemingly stereotyped characters—a technique he was to exploit with some success in *Maestro*. It allows him to insinuate the vulnerability of one such as 'Dad', the seemingly insensitive patriarch, whose certainties are challenged by his encounter with the enemy, the 'bad guys', the centre of the demonology of his class and generation.

His children, the liberated representatives of a new world, one that has no truck with such emblems of stuffy propriety as neckties, reveal a degree of crassness in facets of their personality which are in their own way just as doctrinaire as the older man's. Attitudes and prejudices mingle in this story in a more complex manner than they do in most of the other stories in *Zooing*. There are no comfortable positions to adopt, no certainties to assert. There is, nevertheless, a more compelling sense of the need for tolerance, for the recognition of human values above the ideological, than in the potentially sentimental conclusion, for instance, of 'The Law and Procedure of Meetings in Australia and New Zealand, and I'. Such sentimentality, the danger of kitschiness even, is avoided by the fine control of irony which shows, at the end of 'The Unpleasantness at the Returned Military Officers' Club', that even the narrator, the seemingly humane observer, is capable of sliding back into the self-absorption which provokes the unpleasantness among his family, that emblem of the suburban world these stories explore.

❧

Bleak Rooms, Goldsworthy's third collection of short stories, reveals clearly some of the anxieties that were to become the jesting preoccupations of *Magpie*, that strange exploration of the hazards of the literary life. The location and emphases of the dozen stories that make up the collection are the same as, or at least extensions of, the concerns of the earlier volumes. This is also a world of suburban disasters and betrayals, fictions that test their characters against humanist norms of the kind that were becoming increasingly suspect by the late eighties, the time when this collection was published.

These stories are less clearly—one might even say less mechanically—constructed than Goldsworthy's earlier works in this genre. The scientist's analytical temper, as in the somewhat alarmed confession in the poem 'Credo'—

> *I believe in making lists.*
> *In quartz clocks,*
> *calendars, reminder calls, alarms.*
> *I like the hours 9am and 5pm,*
> *and taking to the weekend shapelessness with these:*
> *hedge-clippers, edge-trimmers,*
> *a lawn-mower on the lowest notch,*
> *secateurs*

—is replaced by more allusive, almost impressionistic structures. Innuendo and implication take the place of the neat ironies, or the careful definition and trimming of many of the earlier stories. These fictions deal with gaps, with the unstated or the unstatable, in structures less precise though possibly more evocative than those encountered in the earlier work.

'Requiescat in Pace', the story that opens the volume, is characteristic of that development. It is among the more oblique of the stories in *Bleak Rooms*. The ten brief, numbered sections convey impressions of a complicated situation and relationship. The narrator finds himself tied, rather unwillingly, to his restless, unhappy sister. Hers is the by now familiar predicament of Goldsworthy's characters—her marriage has broken up, leaving her drifting, dissatisfied. She tries one or another palliative, but returns time after time to seek love or at least compassion from her brother, the narrator, the former scholarship boy whose facility with Latin is for her a source of both continuing pride and resentment. The story ends obliquely, and menacingly, as she returns to Adelaide from a presumably disastrous attempt to make a new life for herself in Sydney:

> *The last time I saw my sister was at her place, after her return.*
> *'If something happens,' she said, 'I want the 23rd Psalm.'*
> *It was a Morning-After: the sun rising on the wreckage of the home-coming party, always a bad time for the human mind. But her tone seemed safely jokey.*
> *'What do you mean, if something happens?'*
> *'If I don't . . . make it.'*
> *'I don't follow.'*
> *'I want the 23rd Psalm at my funeral,' she smiled.*
> *'What funeral?' I asked.*
> *'With a choir, and pipe-organ. I want them all in tears. Or goose-bumps at most. And you David.'*
> *'Yes?'*
> *'I want you to make a speech.'*
> *'Don't be so asinine.'*
> *'I want you to say something in Latin.'*
> *(p. 11)*

Goldsworthy seems to have taken note here of contemporary literary preoccupations. There is no longer even a hint of 'closure', the neat summing up—perhaps trimming down to shape with clippers and secateurs— which characterised those stories in the earlier collections where the narrator usually reaches a measure of understanding, or else registers, with customary irony, the other characters' delusions and fantasies. This is, by contrast, an 'open' ending, with all the disturbing potentialities of such endings. The narrator does not interpret, does not explain, seems content merely to report what he claims to have been his last conversation with his sister. Possibilities, both sinister and risible, are allowed to float freely. This story, like several others in *Bleak Rooms*, seems much closer to the priorities of contemporary practice (and literary theory) than Goldsworthy's earlier works.

That is not to suggest that there is anything merely modish here. The oblique and impressionistic stories in the collection, those where implications emerge from the unstated and the absent, probably reveal as much a concern with the ethical and intellectual implications of this, for Goldsworthy, new mode as with the assertions of literary theory that would deny a writer a control over his material—the type of insistence that is parodied in *Magpie*. These stories seem to suggest that the wellsprings of behaviour cannot be understood as confidently as depicted in the earlier stories—*they* attempted to convey an understanding by means of observing the social and ethical rituals of the suburban world. Though the settings of *Bleak Rooms* are very similar to those in Goldsworthy's earlier collections, and though his characters endure similar trials and betrayals, their tone is generally more ambiguous, often darker; the issues are no longer parcelled or resolved, but often left in a sinister suspension.

'The Affirmative Action Dinner Party' and 'The Nice Chinese Doctor' are both examples of that aspect of *Bleak Rooms*. Each is a third-person narrative, more distanced therefore than the confessional tone of other stories (both here and in the earlier volumes). Each deals with acts of betrayal, or at least of bad faith, which, once more, are implied or suggested, rather than conveyed by the narrator's voice. In the former, the central character's invitation to a neighbour, an environmentalist, to attend a yuppie dinner party ends in disaster and humiliation: after the guest leaves, a sense of desolation descends on him:

> *He lowered his head until he could see nothing but the table: the random clutter of cutlery and smeared plates, the ruined cheese platters, the empty wine-glasses in which difficult stains were already drying. He would be washing them soon, and he felt a sudden, tired disgust, a longing for the tabletop of just a few hours before: that work of organised, symmetrical art, five perfect settings around a circular table, a mandala.*

In the world charted by these stories such neatness and reassurance are no longer available, for the story ends not with those reflections, that sense of futility and dismay, but with an even more cruel recognition:

> *'Perhaps,' he said. 'I wanted her to say the things to* me *that I can't say to myself . . . That I'm too nice to say to myself.'*
> *They all found this very amusing.*
> *'You don't need a stranger to do that,' Cassie said, laughing. 'We'll tell you you're full of shit anytime you ask.'*
> (p. 33)

That double twist, deftly identifying the several layers of betrayal in a mundane, suburban world—for Terry, the central character, is as much betrayed as his guest is betrayed by him—is a darker and more worryingly ambivalent note than Goldsworthy's earlier fiction habitually strikes. It is also heard at the end of 'The Nice Chinese Doctor', when Nick, having achieved his wish that the newly established rival across the street should fail, experiences only bewilderment and desolation:

*Nick returned the receiver slowly to its cradle, then sat for
some time, lost in thought, ignoring his patient. He should
have been happy. No, ecstatic. Instead he felt strangely,
weirdly, empty. He leant his elbows on the desk, and cupped
his face in his hands, thinking.*
(p. 74)

There are one or two stories in *Bleak Rooms* that represent the essentially anecdotal mode of Goldsworthy's earlier collections. Significantly, perhaps, these give an impression of strain, even perhaps of discomfort, which may be taken to suggest that Goldsworthy's interest had moved beyond the anecdotal or the neatly epigrammatic. 'Triple Word Score', a brief story about a recently widowed woman's inability to discuss her future with her son except by means of messages embedded in a game of Scrabble, represents that element in the collection most vividly, but several other stories also seem too neat, too contained for the disturbing and ambiguous situations with which they deal. It might almost seem as if Goldsworthy had become, by the time these pieces were written, dissatisfied with the restriction of a short story, requiring more generous space and scope.

That might indirectly be suggested by the way in which two of the stories in *Bleak Rooms* are linked by incidental and perhaps insignificant details. Terry and Cassie, the hosts of the disastrous 'affirmative action' dinner party, return—at least in name—in the next story in the collection, 'Innocence'. They are different people, precursors of Linda and Rick, the couple at the centre of 'Jesus Wants Me For A Sunbeam'. Terry is married, blissfully it would seem, to Jill. The two are contained within the cocoon of their apparently perfect happiness:

> *there was something closed-off about them, something unitary,*
> *complete, self-contained. They needed no-one—except perhaps*
> *their children. They went nowhere without the latest snapshots*
> *of their children. No dinner-party was allowed to finish before*
> *a handful of these had been passed proudly around.*
> *(p. 39)*

The recently divorced Cassie allows herself to be manoeuvred by friends into a relationship with the narrator, who has also been scarred by a recent separation, and remains 'not completely sane' (p. 37). They decide to live together, though surrounded by suspicion and reluctance:

> *Best of all were the nights. The sex, yes—but more just sitting*
> *around after the children had gone to bed, swapping the day's*
> *stories: the two of us, an oasis of cynicism.*
> *(p. 44)*

They become obsessed by the Blacks' seemingly perfect happiness, and seek opportunities to show them up as shams or—better still—as being just as cynically deracinated as they have become. But the Blacks are impervious. At the end Cassie and the narrator come to the bleak realisation that they are motivated by envy and regret:

> *'I want to believe in them,' she said. 'I only tease them because*
> *I want so much to believe in them.'*
>
> *I felt my eyes fill with tears, my throat tighten. It still felt the*
> *same, exactly, as it had the last time, years and years before,*
> *when I was a child.*
>
> *I pressed myself against her. Outside the rain was falling,*

steadily, smoothly: long ropes of water without end.
  'I want to go back,' she said, wiping away her own tears. 'I want to be like them.'
(p. 47)

There is no suggestion here that 'Innocence' traces the earlier or subsequent history of Cassie and Terry of 'The Affirmative Action Dinner-Party'. The name Cassie had, after all, already made an appearance in the 'The Unpleasantness at the Returned Military Officers' Club'. Yet Goldsworthy is far too conscious a craftsman not to have recognised the implications of placing identically named characters in adjacent stories. A relationship inevitably arises, therefore, between the two. It is not possible to draw conclusions or implications from that conjunction. The conjunction may be no more than a jest, a flourish or even an oversight. Yet it suggests that by the time these stories were written Goldsworthy's imagination needed something more ample than the little 'rooms' of the short story.

Chapter Three

The Fame of the Master

*M*aestro, his first novel, brought Goldsworthy to the attention of a public much larger than the readership of his verse or short stories. The novel's success followed hard on the heels of the original hardback publication in 1989. The paperback appeared in 1990; it was reprinted in the same year, followed by two printings in 1992 and one (at least at the time of writing) in 1993. In the context of 'quality' fiction in Australia, that is a remarkable record for a writer who had previously been known largely as a poet or as a writer of short stories. Several favourable reviews contributed, of course, to that success, but their influence is insufficient to account for the appeal the novel exerted over a public much wider than those who follow reviews in newspapers and periodicals.

This 'rites-of-passage' tale, which begins in steamy Darwin, and retraces its steps to that city via Adelaide and Vienna, brought together the distinctive features of Goldsworthy's preoccupations in his verse and short fiction in a manner enabling them to fulfil their considerable imaginative potential. *Maestro* is a first novel of notable assurance, the work of a writer who had clearly perfected his technique in the series of short stories published over the previous decade or so, and also of a writer who had achieved a clarity and economy of expression and evocation in the small spaces of his sparse and elegant poems; it is a distillation of all he had learnt as a writer.

The novel's opening indicates the manner in which Goldsworthy was now prepared to appropriate the techniques of his verse for the purposes of prose fiction:

> *First impressions?*
>
> *Misleading, of course. As always. But unforgettable: the red glow of his face—a boozer's incandescent glow. The pitted, sun-coarsened skin—a cheap, ruined leather. And the eyes: an old man's moist, wobbling jellies.*
>
> *But then . . . the suit: white linen, freshly pressed. And— absurdly, in that climate—the stiff collar and tie.*
> *(p. 3)*

This the voice of the poet. The grammar is compressed, allowing images and suggestion to stand out sharply, contriving to achieve a precision and specificity without context, self-sufficient, and therefore striking. Indeed, context and the narrative voice—that is to say, the characteristic techniques of Goldsworthy's stories—follow (rather than precede) that impression or sketch of the person we will later come to identify as the Maestro:

> *'Herr Keller?'*
>
> *'Mrs Crabbe?'*
>
> *I stood behind my mother outside his room at the* Swan, *perched on a wooden balcony overlooking the beer garden. The hotel—a warren of crumbling weatherboard, overgrown with bougainvillea—was packed, the drinkers and their noise spilling out of the front bar into the garden. Up the stairs,*

second on the right, a barman had shouted—and every face in
the bar had turned and followed us up. One or two drunken
whistles had also followed us up; whistles living far beyond
their sexual means, my mother later reported to my father,
contemptuously.
(p. 3)

Here is artistry of a high order. The contrivance of the
opening measure of the novel—the musical conceit is once
more by no means irrelevant—is masked by apparent ease
and naturalness. The passages place in juxtaposition two
worlds, and two ways of conveying such worlds, so
providing both the structural and the ethical preoccupations of the novel. Our introduction to Keller, the
Maestro, the mysterious and potentially threatening
'outsider', is by means of the impressionistic fore-
shortening of what is a possibly unconscious appro-
priation of the ancient rhetorical device known as the
blason. A series of vivid descriptions, those misleading
first impressions, convey implications of decadence and
ruin by way of physical characteristics—the leather-like
skin, the 'boozer's incandescent glow', and the disturbing
incompatibility of the freshly pressed linen suit, the stiff
collar and the tie.

Against those impressions, Goldsworthy sets a concrete
and gratingly different world—the familiar, noisy pub, its
raucous drinkers, the frontier vulgarity of Darwin which,
later in the novel, will be contrasted against the glory and
the anguish of Keller's Vienna, and also against the prim
propriety of Adelaide glancingly referred to in Mrs
Crabbe's ironic comments on the denizens of the *Swan*.

For all its seeming ease and naturalness therefore, the
opening of *Maestro* proceeds by way of highly symbolic

means. Here is an equivalent of the careful selection and juxtapositions of Goldsworthy's verse placed within the conventions of prose narrative, specifically of a first-person, coming-of-age story. Keller, who represents both the greatness and the capacity for corruption and suffering in 'European' civilisation, is placed within a typical—though hardly elevated—shrine dedicated to the essence of Australian life: the vulgar, demotic world of the pub. That contrast and juxtaposition provide the shape and emphases for Goldsworthy's exploration of contrasted worlds by means of techniques similar to those he employed in 'Gustav Mahler: Songs on the Death of Children':

> *It's snowing in Adelaide*
> *on the gramophone,*
> *white hiss and static at 78rpm:*
> *snowing in Vienna, in Adelaide.*

The novel, which has something of the quasi-musical structure also apparent in that stanza, achieves a degree of symbolic—one might say poetic—complexity contained within the easy, natural colloquialism of Paul Crabbe's reminiscences of Keller, the leather-faced, alcohol-sodden Maestro in an immaculate linen suit.

❧

Such abstract and complex preoccupations are best approached by way of the natural and the colloquial. The success of *Maestro*, its capacity to appeal to what is obviously a wide readership, relies on the way Goldsworthy has maintained an attractive narrative flow, and an immersion in the characters and their particular, vividly imagined world.

Paul, the narrator, is brought to Darwin by his parents. They have left behind the prim world of Adelaide for the noisy vitality and messy liveliness of pre-cyclone Darwin. Despite being a frontier town with a touch or two of the exotic, Darwin remains, nevertheless, essentially a suburban world. The Crabbes bring with them—as Goldsworthy's parents probably did when they moved to Darwin—a somewhat old-fashioned, rather naïve cultivation that makes them seek out Keller, the exotic Austrian, as a piano teacher for their son, the budding international virtuoso.

Goldsworthy's readers had already encountered the Crabbes, in a slightly different guise, in 'Fall of the Bastille', a story in *Archipelagoes*. Patrick, Paul's avatar, lies 'with his head beneath the piano stool, his mother's feet pressing on the pedals a few centimetres from his ear' (p. 76). Similarly, Paul is forced to endure his parents' attempts to bring culture to raw Darwin, though that culture, as in the case of 'Fall of the Bastille', is no more elevated than amateur productions of Gilbert and Sullivan:

> That June an extra evening was added to my parents' weekly musical calendar: Gilbert and Sullivan night. More musical gipsies than Doctor and Doctor's Wife, they had left a trail of Gilbert and Sullivan performances across the South—a different operetta in every town in which we lived. From an early age I also was involved, if only in lesser, supporting roles. By early teens I had played a pirate in Penzance, a courtier in The Mikado, a juror in Trial By . . .
>
> That simple, stylised music saturates my earliest memories:

> *music first heard from a bassinet beneath my mother's piano in*
> *various small-town Institutes or Church Halls as she rehearsed*
> *the chorus, the squeak of her foot on a pedal close to my ear.*
> *(p. 39)*

The Crabbes have greater ambitions than the provision of Gilbert and Sullivan for whatever town their caravan happens to light on. They sink their disappointments, the dreariness of the life of a country doctor who lacks the ambition and drive of the metropolitan high-flyers of the profession, in fantasies of the cultivated life:

> *Friday night was 'soirée' night. A circle of amateur musicians,*
> *church acquaintances mostly, choir members, began gathering*
> *at our house, each taking turns to prepare and perform some*
> *piece on piano or flute or vocal chord.*
> *(p. 28)*

And they entertain high hopes for Paul's talent and future career despite the fact that weeks of lessons with Keller go by without Paul being allowed to play so much as a note. These hopes come to be severely discouraged when Keller finally accepts the Crabbes' cajoling invitations that he should visit his brilliant pupil's parents:

> *'Perhaps you could play one of the exam pieces, Paul,' my*
> *father suggested. 'A private concert for the three of us.'*
> *'The Brahms?'*
> *'The Beethoven,' Keller interjected, 'might be preferable.'*
> *I played Beethoven that night as well as I had ever played,*
> *and turned afterwards, smiling, ready for praise.*
> *'Beautiful,' my mother breathed. 'Don't you agree Herr*
> *Keller?'*

> *'An excellent forgery,'* he said.
> *'I'm sorry?'*
> *'Technically perfect,'* he said.
> *(pp. 45–6)*

By the end of the novel Paul has come to a realisation of the force of Keller's scathing comment. His attempts at becoming the international virtuoso his parents dream about in steamy Darwin could not be maintained in the face of the 'real' musical world, the European piano-competition circuit where he tries his luck for several dispiriting years. But in Darwin, when Keller speaks those words, and goes on to illustrate his point by describing what he once saw in a museum in Amsterdam—

> *Van Gogh. A fascinating art work. Each violent brush stroke was reproduced with painstaking, non-violent care. The forgery must have taken many times longer than the original to complete. It was technically better than the original . . . And yet something was missing. Not much—but something.*
> *(p. 46)*

—he seems merely rude and deliberately provocative.

Neither Paul nor his parents are prepared to believe him—to them these are merely the words of the curious, drink-sodden foreigner who, for all his elaborately formal manners, treats the cultivated Crabbes with as much disdain as they themselves express towards the denizens of the bar of the *Swan*. They cannot accept the notion that their civilised, music-obsessed life in a raw frontier town is itself as much of an imitation as Paul's well-drilled, technically accomplished but essentially lifeless rendition of one of the great monuments of European musical culture. Goldsworthy's novel reflects, nevertheless, an awareness of the limitations and dangers of such imitative existence, and beyond that, perhaps, an anxiety about the larger implications of pursuing the cultivated life— playing the piano, writing novels—in a world that challenges the validity of such pursuits.

⸎

Some of the generally gentle satire in *Maestro* is centred on the elder Crabbes' attempts to ingratiate themselves with the exotic and alluring Keller.

> *'Shall we eat?' my mother rose from the couch. 'We're having Wiener Schnitzel tonight, Herr Keller. In your honour. And sauerkraut—I had awful trouble finding a recipe.'*
> *. . . 'Vienna,' she continued, determined, 'is my favourite foreign city. I only know it from photographs, of course. The Spanish Riding School. The Ringstrasse . . .'*
> *(p. 45)*

Keller rebuffs these naïve attempts to 'make him feel at home' with savage ill-humour:

> *'The Ringstrasse,' he snorted again. 'Of course. An excellent city for military pomp and processions.'*
> *'But such beautiful architecture.'*
> *'Movie-set architecture,' he murmured. 'Ornamental facades. Hiding the hypocrisy within . . .'*
> *(p. 45)*

Here, within the context of the ironic comedy that distinguishes much of Goldsworthy's fiction, fantasy and experience come into sharp conflict. Keller has reasons, as we learn later, for that jaundiced view of the cultural shrine at which Paul's parents worship, by proxy as it were, when they play Haydn, Mozart and Beethoven on their suburban upright. He cannot share that almost childlike sense of awe before concepts of beauty, grace and civility which are encapsulated for Paul's mother by the magical word 'Vienna'. He knows that the Ringstrasse must be regarded as a site constructed for the display of military and political brutality

In the essentially symbolic world *Maestro* represents—in spite of its apparent naturalness—Paul finds himself torn between rival claims. There is his parents' genteel world of Gilbert and Sullivan performances, their respect for European high civilisation which leads to their ambitions for Paul—ambitions intended as much to compensate for their disappointments as to ensure their son a rich and fulfilled life, as Paul's mother reveals:

> 'Your Father never had your opportunities,' she continued, the words still upper-case and reverential. 'He always regretted it. You must understand: we lost so much time in the War. And after the War there was no time for music. If he seems hard on you, it's because of that.'
> (p. 14)

Paul, true to the desires of adolescents, finds irresistible the opposite of such a genteel, cultivated world. The opening sections of *Maestro*, set in 1967 and 1968, contain clearly-etched impressions of school life at a time when adolescents, for the first time in our social history, were emerging from the tutelage of those values and the propriety that the Crabbes represent in their respect for culture, and for the social codes the respect for culture embodies.

The site for Paul's exploration of less cultivated, demotic possibilities of life is conveyed in terms of the familiar preoccupations of many Australian writers:

> *At first glance it might have been any Southern school: glass boxes squatting in a sea of asphalt, form matched to function. The one concession to latitude was a vast, covered playing area— protection against the tropical rains. On overcast days during the deep Wet, that roofed area entered a kind of steamy twilight. In its dimly lit corners anything became possible. Patterns of experimental behaviour were pioneered that later became widespread: knife-fights, drunkenness, unspeakable acts beneath ping-pong tables. Small beer now, perhaps, accepted as part of the school curriculum everywhere, but at the cutting edge then.*
> *(p. 24)*

In this less than civilised environment Paul explores not merely the world of adolescent sex, or encounters the violence of adrenalin-flooded youths, but also becomes involved in what his parents would regard as the absolute contradiction of all their aspirations—an amateur rock band, propelled to fame by a somewhat fraudulent Darwin disc-jockey. The conflict of those sharply contrasted worlds is contained for Paul within the contrast between Keller's room at the *Swan*, a world of hierarchies, levels, orders—

> *He seated himself at the grand—a* Bösendorfer, *the first I'd seen—and swivelled to face us. The upright—a peeling* Wertheim, *its varnish cracked and bubbled by too many years too near the equator—was mine.*
> *(p. 4)*

and the characteristic emblems of the world of rock:

> *In a far corner, behind a low wall of empty beer bottles, Jimmy*
> *was going through the motions—largely pointless—of tuning*
> *his electric bass. He too had stripped to his waist. His body was*
> *covered with black fur, stiff as steel wool.*
> *(p. 87)*

Even at this stage, it is true, Paul inclines towards the ordered world of the superb *Bösendorfer* and the humble *Wertheim*. When the band performs at a Darwin talent quest, his reactions indicate that preference clearly enough:

> *I loved it at the time: the driving rhythms, the wall of noise, the*
> *carefully cued screams of Rosie and Megan and the rest of our*
> *schoolmates. But, afterwards, sitting there in the spotlight, I*
> *was unable to take it seriously. For one thing, the sheer* hurt *of*
> *the sound we produced always, absurdly, made me want to use*
> *my bowels. The deafening volume seemed to trigger some deep,*
> *physiological reflex. Even then I couldn't help seeing it in those*
> *terms: Music to Shit By.*
> *(p. 91)*

However, Paul is still forced to choose, and the choice is by no means easy. Nor is it unambiguously the correct choice for, as the latter portions of the novel reveal, his essentially imitative attitude to the 'art' of the piano leads to the crumbling of dreams and aspirations. *Maestro* nevertheless affirms the validity of that choice: it is better to have failed in the high demands of 'art' than to have been content to remain among the megadecibel inanities of rock. Or, in a different frame of reference, the Crabbes' naïve and possibly sentimental worship of high culture is nevertheless a finer aspiration than the mindless violence and self-indulgence of the world that finds its location under the roof covering the school playground. That contrast and that choice provide one of the major preoccupations of the novel. They reveal, as well, the consequences of the choice that Goldsworthy exercised, here and also to an extent in his short fiction, about the subject matter and the concerns of his writing.

❧

The steamy world of the roofed schoolyard, the rituals of the pub and the adolescent subculture that began to emerge at the time of the setting of the opening sections of *Maestro*, the late sixties, are familiar aspects of Australian life that have found some representation among contemporary writers. They provide many of the social and political preoccupations of the past twenty years or so. By contrast, the world of suburban propriety, with its respect for European high culture, that Paul's parents bring with them from the 'South' to the vulgarities of Darwin, is often deemed irrelevant to the realities of Australian life at the end of the twentieth century. Yet both *Maestro* and Goldsworthy's work in general declare their fascination with that world in a way that cannot but provide some anxiety or at least misgivings.

The problem Goldsworthy seems to have faced in *Maestro* is related to such social, cultural and even political preoccupations. Should an Australian writer concern himself with matters of European culture and—as it comes to be revealed in the course of the novel—the barbarism that went hand in hand with Europe's worship of its cultural glory? Moreover, even if it should prove proper to engage with experiences that lie outside the confines of Australian life, how does one achieve authenticity, to what extent is it possible to know, to be at ease with worlds as remote from daily life in Australia as the Ringstrasse and The Spanish Riding School? This is, moreover, more than a matter of accuracy, of avoiding the types of howlers that would bring smiles to the faces of European sophisticates. It is a matter of cultural stance, even perhaps of allegiance, which seems particularly to fascinate several writers of Goldsworthy's generation.

Such writers are no longer content to retain their fiction within the traditional concerns of Australian writing of earlier generations. Several recent novelists have tackled 'European' themes of considerable cultural weight—a year or so after *Maestro*, novels were published dealing with, for instance, Evans's excavation of Knossos, and the Wolf-Man, Freud's celebrated patient. *Maestro* is an instance of that phenomenon. Goldsworthy writes with obvious relish about both the physical sites of European musical culture and the culture itself.

In 1975, during his disappointing years of pilgrimage on the piano-contest circuit, Paul travels to Vienna in an attempt to seek out a former colleague of Keller, in order to unravel the secret that seemed to have surrounded the elderly music teacher, a secret Paul had attempted to discover among the music reference books of a library in Adelaide:

> *I had never set foot in the city before, but every street corner brought small shocks of rediscovery, realisations of things I hadn't known I knew: the familiar features of that dream city of music and dusty history which I had put together in my head from books, in the Library of the University of Adelaide*

many years before. I wandered through the Staatsoper, the
Rathaus, the maze of the Wiener Hofburg, needing no tour-
guide but myself . . .

Henisch, the cellist, lived in a small third-floor apartment in
Neubau, on Mariahilfer Strasse. (I write these placenames
casually, as if I had lived among them all my life—and in many
senses I have lived among them all my life.)
(p. 133)

These places and their resonance are familiar not merely
to the protagonist; they have entered into the fabric of the
novel's—and obviously of Goldsworthy's—imagination
by way of the easy familiarity it reveals with the musical
glories produced by those monuments of marble and
stone. They provide an environment more congenial than
the noisy vulgarity of the *Swan*, the sordid world beneath
the roof slung over the Darwin schoolyard, or even
perhaps the Crabbes' rather indiscriminate attempts to
emulate such cultural achievements by way of serving
sauerkraut and schnitzel.

There is, nevertheless, the problem of perspective and
the problem of propriety. Is it possible to appropriate that
world from the perspective of what would, for that world
at least, be deemed the antipodes? How to avoid the
potential foolishness or even vulgarity of one like Paul's
mother, who imagines that her no doubt feeble attempts
at Austrian cuisine might ingratiate her with Keller, the
echt Austrian? Those conundrums give particular weight,
even perhaps sonority to *Maestro* in its exploration of the
difference between fantasies of European civilisation—as
entertained by the elder Crabbes, and embodied in their
attempts to emulate that civilisation—and the truth of
what lies behind that civilisation, which Paul discovers in

his journey towards personal and cultural maturity. *Maestro*, by means of its exploration of Paul's infatuation with a world far removed from his experiences of life, represents a way of comprehending such preoccupations within a coherent and intellectually responsible work of fiction.

Someone such as Paul—who is in some limited sense obviously Goldsworthy's alter ego—must always remain an outsider in that world, essentially a tourist, no matter how deep the cultural dedication to it might be:

> *I was beached in Europe at the time, stranded between one competition and the next. On Rosie's advice I had visited Salzburg; trekked through the winter snows from various Birthplaces to Performances to Gravestones, more out of obligation to her and to my parents—who were still footing the bill, and who used me as a surrogate tourist—than for myself.*
> (p. 131)

That world cannot be known with intimacy, and it cannot therefore be written about, except from the perspective of someone who is, at best, on its margins—unless, that is, both writer and fictional character attempt the possibly futile task of merging into that other, alien world.

At the narrative level of *Maestro*, Paul decides to do precisely that. When he accedes to his parents' fantasies concerning his potentially brilliant career as an international piano virtuoso—indeed a 'maestro'—he is deliberately turning his back on the world that had been most familiar to him: dank Darwin, the covered schoolyard, the rituals of the *Swan*. Moreover, he also turns his back on the other part of his heritage, so to speak—genteel Adelaide and his parents' worship of high culture—which might seem at first blush closer to the world of European priorities than to the raucous vulgarity of Darwin. Yet that world too has to be discarded, just as the prospect of a decent profession, a steady, sensible life, must be sacrificed to the dreams and illusions that initially led Paul into his brush with a representative of European culture in a room above one of Darwin's many pubs. The section of *Maestro* entitled '1974' begins, accordingly, as follows:

> *The years that followed in Adelaide, at the Conservatorium,*
> *passed so slowly, so monotonously, that the retelling of them*
> *can only pass quickly. My Law studies soon fell by the*
> *wayside—early successes encouraged me to concentrate on*
> *Music instead. I left a trail of prizes behind me . . . and also a*
> *trail of teachers. Keller had spoiled me, I soon began to realise. I*
> *quickly tired of the second-rate, and the first-rate tired equally*
> *quickly of me and my rigid second-hand opinions.*
> (p. 123)

He has been bitten by the bug of the exotic. All that he associates with—or entertains fantasies about—the drink-sodden 'genius' of the room above the *Swan*, seems hostile and alien to the humdrum world of the everyday, whether in Adelaide or Darwin. So strong indeed is that allure that it transcends Paul's fascination with Keller, the representative of that beguiling world. When Keller writes to Paul in Adelaide—half as supplicant, half as *grand seigneur*—inviting him to spend Christmas with him to learn more Bach, Paul chooses (perhaps sensibly) the charm of spending the season with Rosie. Yet Keller's influence proves irrestistible; the dream he unwittingly implanted in Paul beckons. Though the signs are there clearly enough that his dedication to music is more emotional than fundamental, that the second-ratedness is within him, not within the world in which he is forced to live, Paul leaves for Europe to pursue a great career, but also, or so the novel suggests, to achieve contact with those cultural and perhaps even spiritual potentialities that the notion of 'Europe' represents for cultivated Australians of Goldsworthy's generation.

And so it is with the larger project of the novel itself. Goldsworthy too is drawn to a world in which an Australian writer, no matter how cosmopolitan (or 'Eurocentric') in outlook, must remain an alien and an outsider. This is not a matter so much of 'Australianness', that is of a deliberate, even perhaps aggressive, chauvinism, as of lack of familiarity, and the consequent difficulty of writing about societies, places, cultural rituals and the like which one cannot experience at first hand or closely. For that reason, perhaps, where Australian writers of Goldsworthy's generation have dealt with 'The Matter of Europe' (as in the case of Brian Castro for instance) the tendency has been towards fantasy, towards conjuring at times surrealistic images of 'Europe'. That is not Goldsworthy's way; his fiction is too far embedded in an essentially realistic (or perhaps naturalistic) mode for such a device to be possible. Rather, the anxieties of a writer who is drawn to that subject matter and finds there the source of both inspiration and reluctance to pursue it, have to be contained within the narrative itself, within the characters, their predicaments and the world they inhabit. *Maestro* reveals, indeed, precisely such an accom-modation, such an attempt to quell the alarm of writing about the 'outside', the unknown or at least only superficially known.

❧

Maestro is primarily concerned with Eduard Keller, the European virtuoso who has fetched up in the frontier society of Darwin; a grotesque figure in a carefully pressed white suit and panama hat, a drunkard and an outcast recalling those sad and sinister individuals who wander around the 'Far East' in Conrad's and Somerset Maugham's stories. Paul's journey towards discovering his own mediocrity—and also towards coming to terms with it—is in many ways merely a casing for the novel's exploration of the paradox of Keller: he is a broken-down representative of all that people like the Crabbes worship from afar, and therefore a means of permitting Goldsworthy to locate the novel's most telling emphases on that alien, 'other world' from which Keller had emerged. Just as Paul is obliged to discover the 'truth' about Keller in a tentative and circuitous fashion, so Goldsworthy seems to approach the core of his concern— the implications of the fantasies of Europe that sustain people such as Paul's parents—obliquely, with care and perhaps even with a measure of anxiety. The knowledge gained by the end of the novel, which confounds the categories of fantasy and prejudice entertained by the Crabbes and their like, is as painful and as lacking in romance or mystery as Paul's own recognition of his own lack of status and potential as a maestro.

For much of the novel Keller remains an enigma. The people of Darwin suspect that he has an unsavoury past; others wonder whether he is a fraud, a charlatan who exploits the ignorance and lack of sophistication of those whom he both impresses and scandalises with his airs and foreign ways. Is he a former Nazi fleeing from the consequences of horrors he may have committed or condoned, to an obscure place which Paul's father thinks of as another 'arsehole of the earth'? Interestingly, 'arsehole of the earth' is a phrase often used to describe Auschwitz, the site of those terrible outrages Keller is suspected by some of having committed:

Various theories, half-truths and slanders were bruited about,
often totally contradictory, and always extreme. My own
former theory was even aired by others: he was a War Criminal
in hiding. More often he was Jewish, an Auschwitz survivor.
Or a Russian, a Trotskyite. Sometimes he had a criminal
record: postwar black market, forged Deutschmarks. Or he had
worked the pearling luggers, made a fortune, filtered it through
his kidneys . . .
(p. 29)

Such is the impact of his otherness, that is his foreignness, that he comes to be both romanticised and feared. Paul's mother attempts to propitiate him with Wiener schnitzel and sauerkraut, as though he were a minor god. Similar rites are played out in Adelaide where Keller accompanies Paul to assist in his training for a piano competition:

Grandmother Wallace was most taken with her Continental
Gentleman and his gruffly formal manners. Breakfast was the
only meal he shared with us, and she soon determined to make
the most of it: to lift it beyond the realm of the daily and the
mundane. I could set from memory a replica of the perfect Still

Life she laid out on the table each morning: the carefully folded
Advertiser; *the two canary yellow hemispheres of grapefruit*
in their bowls, separated by a more richly yellowed cube of
butter; the sky blue milk-jug and matching sugar bowl filled to
the brim with their differently textured whitenesses; the pot of
tea snug in its knitted navy blue cosy, the steam that rose
invisibly from its spout suddenly rendered visible, swirling,
where it entered the slanting morning light.
(pp. 100–01)

None of this solicitousness pacifies the maestro; he
remains a creature of mystery and menace. Mrs Wallace
misinterprets his obsessive interest in newspapers, the
source of those sinister, faded cuttings commemorating
the world's idiocy and outrages the boy Paul discovers
one day in the room above the *Swan*.

'I can see you are a kindred spirit,' my grandmother told him,
scrabbling to find common interests, or some shared language.
'I can't seem to get started in the morning without my
Advertiser.'
'I loathe all newspapers,' Keller assured her. 'The goitre of the
world, a friend of mine once described them. But we must
study the goitre, carefully. Like doctors. Pathologists.'
(p. 103)

Neither Darwin nor Adelaide can guess the source of
such obsession, because those worlds—which represent in
many ways the world in which Goldsworthy must locate
his novels and stories—know little of the anguish or the
brutality that bred Keller's obsession and despair. One of
the great strengths of Goldsworthy's careful, almost
minimalist construction in *Maestro* is the way in which the

reader is inducted into recognising that beneath the eccentricity, the arrogance and unpredictability of the old boozer in the white linen suit lurks a figure of tragic proportions. The disclosure of those proportions follows the path of the Crabbes' uncomprehending attempts to discover Keller's secret.

It is of course a secret none of them suspects. For them he is either a romantic genius or a fraud. Their attempts to reconstruct his past from scattered and ambiguous fragments is always predicated upon the supposition of some dark, perhaps heroic secret, or else on the suspicion that he was 'putting one over' the isolated world of Darwin in the sixties. 'He must be pulling your leg' (p. 20) is the comment Paul's father makes on learning that Keller claimed to have been taught by one of Liszt's pupils. His scepticism is turned into almost blind faith when an allusion to Keller is found in a music reference book. His dry comment 'Must be a common name, Keller . . . The Smiths of Austria' (p. 20) is soon converted into:

> '*It might not be the same man,*' *my mother reminded him, her own excitement waning a little as if in counterweight to his. 'Leschetizky probably had any number of students called Keller.'*
>
> *But my father wanted to believe.*
>
> '*Eduard Keller?*' *he said. 'The coincidence is too great.'*
> (p. 21)

Indeed they all want to believe. They want to believe that he is a war criminal, someone with a romantic or colourful past. They interpret the 'evidence'—a faded photograph, the assertion of music authorities that Eduard Keller, the famous Viennese virtuoso, did not survive the war—in ways that would bolster up their fantasies and their conviction that whatever deed Keller might have been guilty of was bound to be more glamorous, more heroic perhaps, than the possibilities offered by life in vulgar Darwin or prim Adelaide.

In short, Goldsworthy's characters—or at least Paul and his family—exhibit that habitual self-denigration, that unquestioned assumption that what happens *there*, in Europe, in the old world, is more interesting and more dramatic than anything their humdrum lives can offer. At a fundamental level *Maestro* is concerned with self-image and self-esteem, and with the attempts of at least older Australians to define themselves and their society by reference to the remote and the external which provided fantasies they accepted as real. The novel is concerned with displaying the folly of engaging in such deprecating self-definition, but then—with a twist characteristic of Goldsworthy's fictional practices—it also reveals how that 'other', the fabulous world of Europe which had been worshipped by generations of Australians such as the Crabbes and lovingly passed on by them to their children, does indeed contain experiences undreamt of in the protected world of modern Australia. The bleak irony at the heart of the novel states that there is nothing fabulous or glamorous about such otherness, merely a potential for brutality and suffering that most Australians have not experienced at first hand.

These strands come together, late in the novel, when Paul tracks down Henisch the cellist, one of Keller's former colleagues, in his dark, varnished flat in Vienna. Paul learns that Keller's past was different from the romantic fantasies they had entertained in that other 'arsehole of the earth'. Henisch reveals a Keller who was a mixture of the heroic and the banal, the diabolic and the altruistic, in a manner unexpected and undreamt of. Yes, he collaborated with the Nazis after the *Anschluss* of 1938, but his collaboration was venal, confused, based on the foolish belief that his good standing with the regime would save his Jewish wife and son. Paul then learns about his terrible remorse, and about an act of expiation and self-sacrifice that Paul's world finds difficult to comprehend. When his wife and child—the child could have been saved but refused to be separated from his mother—were taken away, Keller died, according to Henisch:

> *'I'm sorry?'*
>
> *'He sewed the yellow star to his clothing on his return to Vienna. He registered as a Jew.'*
>
> *I seemed to be learning too much too quickly. As he spoke each astonishing sentence I was still grappling with some previous astonishing sentence.*
>
> *'But Keller was not Jewish,' I tried to keep up.*
>
> *'He no longer wished to be Austrian. He was transported in 1942.'*
>
> *'I don't understand. He* pretended *to be Jewish? He* wanted *to be transported?'*
>
> *Henisch sipped silently at his lemon-scented tea in its frail, exquisite cup.*
>
> *'Some form of penance?' I guessed, trying to wrap my mind around it. 'Self-punishment?'*
> *(pp. 136–7)*

But none of these categories approximate to the 'truth' as Henisch sees it from his different perspective, from that world which had been, hitherto, a source of romantic

fantasies for the Crabbes. For him, Keller's history is like
the history of countless confused people who were caught
up in the madness of a world they could neither control
nor understand. And, he insists, Keller died in 1945,
during the terrible forced marches the Germans imposed
on the surviving inmates of concentration camps as the
Russian army advanced on Central Europe.

For him, Keller is dead; nothing the young Australian,
from a world fabulously remote in his eyes, says is
capable of convincing him that Keller may have survived
or, in a way, resurrected himself at the other end of the
earth. He remains sceptical even when Paul produces his
trump card as it were, the strange, seemingly scandalous
physical peculiarity of Keller, which had caused so much
comment and conjecture in Darwin:

> *'How can I convince you? He always wears white. He has a
> finger missing from the right hand.'*
>
> *He glanced up at me curiously, and I pressed on:*
> *'I'm right, aren't I? He had no little finger?'*
> *'Eduard had ten fingers. Of course. He was a pianist.'*
> *He paused, his eyes becoming glazed, unfocused; or tuning
> perhaps to some different, internal focal length.*
> *'But I remember,' he murmured. 'In the camps. There was a
> piano in the SS mess. A guard once asked him to play. Of
> course he refused—even if they killed him he wouldn't play.
> But afterwards he told me . . .that if he ever felt the desire to
> play again he would hack off his fingers, one by one.'*
> *(p. 138)*

Yet Henisch will not accept Paul's triumphant assertion:
'Then it *is* him'. He assures the excited young man that
the teacher who had trained him in faraway Darwin did

not prefer Bach and Mozart to the 'empty rhetoric' of the Romantics:

> *'Eduard Keller would never play Mozart if he could play Liszt,*
> *or Rachmaninoff. He liked to entertain. He liked a big, strong*
> *sound.'*
> *(p. 138)*

And, moreover, when Paul makes a final attempt to prove his point by playing a piece Keller had taught him, Henisch is confirmed in his certainty:

> *'Very fine,' he murmured as I slipped my hands from the*
> *keyboard, the sound of the last chords lingering there like a pair*
> *of forgotten gloves. 'Technically flawless. You obviously had a*
> *very fine teacher. But I am sorry: you did not learn from*
> *Eduard Keller . . .'*
> *(p. 139)*

To prove his point, he gives Paul a precious gift, Keller's last recording, made in 1934, containing two pieces by Liszt, the arch romantic, the prince of showy piano virtuosos of the kind that Paul's teacher had regarded with scathing scorn.

'Perhaps his Keller had died long before mine was born' (p. 140) Paul thinks at the end of his painful, enigmatic interview with Henisch the cellist. In that way Goldsworthy spells out, perhaps a trifle too emphatically, the paradox at the heart of *Maestro*.

The end of the novel does nothing to resolve these mysteries in any literal, or perhaps forensic, sense. In 1977 Paul—

> *greying, dissatisfied, fast approaching mid-life, my backside*
> *stuck fast to a minor chair in a minor music school. Able to*
> *dupe my audiences at the odd concert, and even the critics—*
> *no, especially the critics—but never for one moment, even at*
> *my most unguarded, deluding myself*
> *(p. 148)*

—is summoned to a reborn Darwin because Keller, who had survived an apocalypse in both hemispheres, is at the point of death. He sits with the old man, attempting to comfort him, but also teasing away at the conundrum— was this Keller, the remote, emotionless advocate of the purity of music the same as the romantic virtuoso who had recorded in 1934 the music of the high priest of keyboard romanticism? He finds no answer, but the end of the novel suggests an understanding, and more importantly a recognition that Keller too had changed, evolved and had also come to terms with disappointment (and worse) in the way that Paul has had to come to terms with his own mediocrity.

Maestro deals therefore with varieties of transformation. Keller, the survivor, the voluntary outcast and exile in a place least resembling Vienna, that treacherous shrine of Central European culture, has remade himself (or has allowed himself to be remade) into his opposite. The romantic has been converted into the ascetic and the cynic. Paul and the reader come to understand that what had seemed like arrogance—such as his socially embarrassing behaviour in Darwin at an open-air concert given by a visiting symphony orchestra—was merely one layer of the protective armour he had arranged around himself. Coldness is recognised as anguish; brusqueness (especially towards Paul, the tormented pupil) as a species of love. Paul and Keller are, according to the resonant suggestions embedded in the novel's final sections, two halves of the one entity. Each has to come to terms with the gulf between illusion and the true state of the world—cataclysmically in Keller's case, with much more gentle effect for Paul. The novel ends, therefore, with a question and an affirmation, as applicable, in their ways, to Keller as they are to Paul:

> *Can I know that mine was a foolish, innocent world, a world of*
> *delusion and feeling and ridiculous dreams—a world of*
> *music—and still love it?*
> *Endlessly, effortlessly.*
> (p. 149)

❧

Despite its brevity, *Maestro* is rich with cultural, psychological and even perhaps political and spiritual implications. In a manner characteristic of Goldsworthy's short stories it considers issues of considerable moment obliquely and allusively—in the way, incidentally, in which poetry (including some of Goldsworthy's) habitually considers such issues. *Maestro* is concerned therefore, at its most abstract level, with the nature of Australian life in the middle of the twentieth century, with the fantasies and aspirations of many of the inhabitants of that 'new world', and with the painful recognition such a world is forced to endure about the source of its fantasies and aspirations when it is obliged to confront one such as Keller, the outcast, the driven creature. That clash of cultures and experiences, the collision of dreams and longings almost, is perceived in the novel, moreover, as being part of a larger movement in Australian society (or culture for that matter) in the years in which Paul's 'getting of wisdom' took place—a movement which replaced the certainties of people like Paul's parents with the much more troubling, but perhaps healthier world of contemporary Australia's eclectic richness of traditions and pursuits.

For all that, the singular achievement of *Maestro* is the containment of such issues in a very particular, autonomous world peopled by characters who strike the reader as individuals, not as pawns in a social or cultural chess game. Goldsworthy's technique relies strongly on implication. His vividly imagined worlds—the humid chaos of Darwin, the few privileged glimpses we have of Adelaide, perhaps the most 'proper' of Australian cities, the Europe Paul sees with antipodean eyes—contain resonances that lead us to recognise those larger implications in an essentially poetic manner. These implications are buried within the particularity of a clearly etched world with such precision that to extract them or to extrapolate from them would seem to be almost improper and excessive.

Yet within the precisely and lovingly observed trivia that seem to fill much of the novel, these resonances and implications are nevertheless clearly recognisable. The main reason why they remain so is a consequence of the careful, essentially *symbolic* construction of *Maestro*, a highly contrived structure which merely conveys a sense of random events, personalities and attitudes.

Such careful, poetic construction is apparent in the novel's time-frame. The decade from 1967 to 1977, in which Paul achieves both disillusionment and a measure of maturity, coincided with major changes in the fabric and nature of Australian society, some of which had come about through the impact people such as Keller had made on that society. That time-frame allows Goldsworthy nevertheless to explore certain essentially abstract patterns that allow this 'rites-of-passage' story to convey implications much beyond the customary concerns of such fiction.

The novel comes to an end as Paul attends the dying Keller's bedside in a Darwin recently reconstructed after the terrible destruction of Cyclone Tracy. That epilogue-like passage is placed into close juxtaposition with an account of Paul's meeting with the cellist Henisch in Vienna, a city that had experienced its own cataclysm and had endured patiently loving reconstruction. Those events frame, in a way rich with implications that cannot be spelt out literally, the tale of death, rebirth and a second death that Keller, perhaps a latter-day Flying Dutchman, endures in two hemispheres. His life in each of those hemispheres, moreover, seems to be the reverse image of the other, catching several almost mythic possibilities that emerge out of Goldsworthy's seemingly easy-going, naturalistic tale.

In the manner of a poet, too, he uses images (or symbols in the way poetry rather than symbolism understands the word) that echo and reverberate through the narrative, setting up nodes, points of contact out of which (once again) richly suggestive, though by no means precise, meanings may emerge. One such example, perhaps the most telling, is the manner in which Henisch's revelation about Keller, the arch romantic who worshipped the music of the Romantics (Liszt, Wagner, Rachmaninoff), is prefigured when, in 1968, Paul, climbing the steps leading to the room above the *Swan*—the name itself suggesting, perhaps, a Wagnerian motif—overhears Keller playing and singing music which contradicts all the principles he had attempted to instil in his pupil:

I knew the piece well; Wagner again. My father often played orchestral excerpts from Tristan *on his gramophone. But I had never heard it played quite like this: a piano transcription, accompanied by snorts of contemptuous laughter, and phrases of angry, broken singing.*

There was passion in the voice, yes, but under immense pressure: a passion that was given in hints, then snatched away, given again, and disallowed again . . .
(p. 73)

Paul might forget the hints given (and perhaps snatched away) in that account of Keller's playing and singing which conveys 'a rapture beyond anything I had ever heard', but the reader does not. We remember the discovery Paul and his mother made, the previous year, in their attempt to exhaust the resources of a library in Adelaide for details of Keller's life. There they learn that 'the Austrian pianist could not save [his wife] the celebrated Jewish contralto and Wagner specialist, Mathilde Rosenthal, who died in Auschwitz, probably in 1942' (p. 56). And we recall the day Paul climbed the stairs to the room above the *Swan* when Henisch, years later, makes him a gift of Keller's precious 1934 recording of Liszt's transcription of the *Tristan* Liebestod. Such resonances confer emotional and intellectual distinction on what many regard to be Goldsworthy's finest achievement so far.

Chapter Four

Raising the Dead

*M*aestro is linked in a number of important ways with Goldsworthy's short stories. Each of the seven sections of that short novel is centred on a particular stage in Paul's development from adolescence to maturity, from being a victim of illusions to reaching a reconciliation with his fundamental, all too human mediocrity. From those vantage points the history of Eduard Keller is reconstructed in a largely oblique and allusive manner. The central concern of the novel—signalled by its title—does not lie at the centre of its narrative structure. Goldsworthy's procedure, as in his short stories, is largely anecdotal and oblique. Even the significant stages in Paul's life, his marriage to Rosie for instance, are fleetingly presented by retrospect. Though there is a narrative strand in *Maestro*, the construction does not reveal a significant narrative flow. The novel's intensity and power emerge from its disclosures of Paul's discoveries, both about himself and about his drink-sodden piano teacher.

When it was published late in 1992, Goldsworthy's second novel, *Honk If You Are Jesus*, disappointed some of his readers by its much less intense tone and by its apparent investment of energies in an entertaining narrative. To many it seemed not much more than a wry fantasy, a lively satire on a clutch of contemporary

81

preoccupations—revivalist Christianity, the glitz of the Gold Coast, the obsessions of those at the cutting edge of scientific inquiry. It is all that. Yet beneath its liveliness and fun, the novel reveals an engagement with issues as pressing as those explored in *Maestro*, though articulated in a much more consecutive structure, a structure which owes more to certain familiar traditions of the novel than to the essentially anecdotal nature of the short story as reflected in the construction of *Maestro*.

At the time of its publication, *Honk If You Are Jesus* was a futuristic fantasy. Several cunningly scattered clues reveal that the climax of the story is reached around July 1994: at the time of writing this was the near future, the twenty-fifth anniversary of the first landing on the moon. Yet in that narrow time-span, Goldsworthy depicts a world which has been fundamentally changed by the rush of scientific discovery and exploration.

❧

The career of Mara Fox, a middle-aged, disillusioned, bored gynaecologist, seems to have run into a dead-end. She spends her life in an Adelaide hospital performing minor obstetrical procedures. Her research into *in vitro* fertilisation has all but ground to a halt through funding cuts and the indifference of bureaucratic institutions. She has no life outside of the hospital. Her mother has long ago abandoned any hope that Mara might marry and give birth to a child. Nor has Mara ever entertained a desire for anything other than the world of the hospital and the laboratory. Yet, as the novel opens, she is the victim of a particularly potent *ennui,* even though it offers her a necessary protection; a way, ultimately, of keeping the more distracting aspects of life at arm's length:

Administration now swallowed much of my time, but even the
clinical work had become a grind: entire theatre lists of
hysterectomies, entire lists of wedge resections. Entire lists of
abortions. I had always loved this world: the world of the
operating theatre. Inhuman describes it best, some claim, but it
is the world I most trust: the sterile corridors, the scrubbed
floors and walls, the stainless-steel trays and trolleys. It's a
world without feeling or ornament, a world stripped to a
utilitarian minimum, where forms are matched perfectly to
functions . . .
(p. 17)

Honk If You Are Jesus explores the moral, social and
psychological implications of such dedication to science,
and also of that retreat into the mysteries of a profession
that once sustained Mara. It is a world Goldsworthy had
already explored in his short stories and in poetry in the
sinister implications of 'Credo':

> *I believe in the infinite line,*
> *the straight line between points*
> *and the equality of all right angles.*
> *Amen.*

The novel gives these concerns an extended and lively
embodiment in Mara's adventures on the Gold Coast of
the near future, where the ethical implications of that kind
of scientific spirit are tested. But it does more; it takes
Goldsworthy's concerns with such matters one step
further, into an area not much explored in contemporary
fiction, yet an area already hinted at in the poem
expressing the scientist's creed.

Mara is rescued from the dreary routines of the
obstetrics ward, and from the suffocating boredom of her

life in the Adelaide suburbs, by an invitation to take up the position of a professor in a medical school on the Gold Coast. The school has been established by Hollis Schultz, a revivalist preacher, the tsar of a mega-enterprise, who is able to guarantee unlimited funds for her research into human reproduction. The earlier sections of the novel reveal a lively, though essentially good-natured, satire of the idiocies of commercialised religion.

Dominating the environs of the Hollis Schultz University is the 'famous Rose Cathedral', as it is called by Mara's guide when she is taken on the obligatory guided tour:

> *A bus-load of Japanese tourists had disgorged on to the*
> *cathedral steps; I had no wish to join them. Apart from the*
> *colour—pink marble—the building looked like a scaled down,*
> *Disney imitation of the cathedral of Notre Dame of Paris. Of*
> *course it possessed none of the character of the original. There*
> *was something too smooth about it, too new; it had none of the*
> *million-fold defects and weatherings and eccentric orna-*
> *mentations that accumulate like barnacles around great*
> *buildings over long periods of time.*
> *(pp. 35–6)*

Despite her scepticism, despite the fact that she had abandoned religion in her adolescence—when her father, a preacher, could not resolve to her satisfaction the paradoxes and conundrums of Christianity—Mara finds herself drawn to this dotty world. She is attracted, of course, by the siren song of unlimited research oppor-tunities, by the prospect of being freed from the dreary routine of the public health system. Her rational self is contemptuous of the blarney of Schultz's revivalism, of the Lego cathedral, of the Lake of Galilee on which one may easily walk thanks to a sturdy sheet of fibreglass placed a centimetre or two below the surface. But as she begins to enjoy the privileges of her new-found status, she is drawn imperceptibly into the influence of Schultz and of Mary-Beth, his young, naïve, simpering wife whom Mara dubs 'Miss Tennessee' in commemoration of her giving the impression of having been a finalist in a beauty contest. And she is drawn to the extraordinary potentiality for the brave new world of scientific discovery that this fundamentalist institution offers—even though she does not pause to consider the anomaly of such an institution's engaging in the latest tricks of genetic engineers.

One of the prize exhibits in the biblical theme park erected around Schultz's domain is a Noah's ark, where 'pairs of tame animals—sheep, goats, Shetland ponies, extravagantly-plumed fowls—wandered freely ...'. Nearby she finds:

> *Two large flightless birds were plodding awkwardly through the leaves and twigs that carpeted their cage, raking food-scraps from time to time with absurdly shaped beaks.*
> *A nearby hoarding identified the species, but I had no need of it.*
>   Raphus cucullatus. Previously extinct. Original
>   habitat Mauritius and adjacent islands. This pair
>   donated to Schultz University by Dr William Scanlon,
>   Stanford University.
> *(p. 43)*

This is the legendary dodo, extinct for four hundred years, which had been resurrected, from scraps of specimens preserved in museums around the world, by Scanlon, the *wunderkind* of genetic magicians in the heady world of the near future Goldsworthy conjures in this novel.

Mara finds, after taking up her prestigious Chair in

Human Reproduction, that Scanlon, a scruffy, pint-sized individual for whom personal hygiene is low in priority, has also been lured to the Gold Coast by Schultz's extraordinary ability to entice the most glittering stars in the scientific firmament. And she also finds that she is drawn into curious experiences and relationships that challenge both her professional and emotional convictions.

Scanlon, childish in his apparent relish for resurrecting long-extinct species with his wizardry, successfully brings back to life the Tasmanian tiger and, half-seriously, wonders whether he ought to have a go at something like the mammoth. Mara joins in the game with enthusiasm— what surrogate mother would carry the embryo: an elephant? a whale? She is less impressed by Scanlon's other preoccupation, a delving around in the murky world of religious relics.

Schultz has collected, from reliquaries scattered around the world, remnants of Christ's Passion: fragments of the nails of the Cross, of St Veronica's cloth, of the Shroud, congealed drops of the True Blood, in short those insignia of superstitious mumbo-jumbo which the scientific mind should shun and despise. After her first visit to the White House, the Schultzes' Hollywood-inspired mansion that dominates the grounds of the university, Mara is taken on a tour of the holy of holies, an oppressive, heavily guarded room where these treasures are kept. Dr Grossman, a cadaverous historian, inducts the Schultzes' guests into the mysteries:

The drawers slid open; the boxes were removed. We were permitted to examine an assortment of objects, some no more than a single crumb of rust, others in better condition: a collection that resembled the odd nails and metal scraps that

might be found in a carpenter's oddments box left out too long
in the rain.
(p. 117)

Goldsworthy's writing conveys with admirable restraint and allusiveness Mara's mixed reactions—the scientist's scorn for superstitious mumbo-jumbo mingled with a fascination she finds hard to control.

Scanlon, she discovers, is also fascinated by this detritus of the Passion. As the guests shuffle reverentially into the claustrophobic reliquary, she is surprised to come upon him installed there with the paraphernalia of his craft.

Grossman also seemed surprised: 'Working Sundays, Professor
Scanlon?'
  'Nothing better to do.'
  'This seems a bit out of your province,' I said, approaching.
  He shifted his body slightly; was he deliberately obscuring
the objects on the bench?
  'I take an interest,' he murmured.
(pp. 115–6)

Yet it is only much later that she is able to comprehend why Scanlon, with his essential scepticism, indeed with his patent unconcern for the consequences of his research, should spend his Sundays entombed with such cult objects.

Mara reaches that understanding only after she comes to learn to what extent she has been used and duped by Schultz, by Scanlon—who awakens in her a sexuality she thought she did not possess—and even by her closest associate, Tad, the opera-loving, 'deviant' embryologist. She realises that the glittering prize she had been offered out of the blue had little to do with the fame or significance of her research work into infertility in purely scientific terms. She had been hired, she learns, in order to allow the childlike Mary-Beth to carry Schultz's child.

Her task seems insurmountable, for it is Schultz, not the child-bride, who is infertile, or so Mara is led to believe. The vast and vastly expensive medical institution in the Disneyworld of the Gold Coast proves to have but one aim: to allow the spermless Schultz to have his genetic material manufactured into a type of pseudo-sperm to impregnate the ova Mara removes with lovingly precise care from Mary-Beth's ovaries. That poses the predictable ethical dilemma:

> *I had no objection to working for faith-healers. I even had no*
> *objection to working for faith-healers who didn't believe in*
> *what they were doing. If anything, I had warmed to the Jekyll*
> *and Hyde flip-sides of Hollis Schultz. Where my research*
> *funding came from was no concern of mine as long as it*
> *arrived on schedule and provided I was granted a free hand.*
> *But a new problem had surfaced: how free was it?*
> *(p. 126)*

That dilemma forces Mara to flee from the Gold Coast back to the stuffy confinement of her widowed mother's house in Adelaide, where she finds to her surprise that that elderly matron, seemingly trapped within the proprieties of that world from which many of the younger characters in Goldsworthy's short stories strive to escape, has taken in a lover.

Mara also finds that her judgement is coloured by her growing fascination with, indeed potential love for, the scruffy Scanlon, despite his pungent male smell, filthy shirts and childlike irresponsibility. The code of ethics whereby she conducts her life, the scientist's fondly held belief in independence, which is ultimately a claim of self-sufficiency and self-determination, is challenged when she learns about Schultz's motives in offering her her lucrative and glamorous position. She rationalises, therefore, her own complicity when she decides to return to the Gold Coast, in the same way that she might be seen to have rationalised, or perhaps swept under the carpet, the considerable ethical dilemmas of abortion, because she believed that abortion was 'Every woman's right' (p. 12). Such convictions are tested when Mara is forced to realise that in Queensland she has not been acting with scientific detachment, as she had believed, because she is being manipulated by others for their own purposes. And that, in terms of the subtle suggestiveness of *Honk If You Are Jesus*, is particularly distressing for her since it denies her her god-like self sufficiency and self-determination in questions of morality and ethics.

That dilemma is, of course, pertinent to the fundamentally secular means whereby such questions are discussed and evaluated in contemporary society. The curious distinction of this novel is that by means of this clever, satirical fable of the near future, Goldsworthy obliges his readers to consider—no matter how tentatively or hypothetically—the religious implications of such attitudes and convictions.

e~

The dilemma at the heart of the novel—to what extent is it justifiable to interfere with the processes of nature, of conception and birth and to bring about the resurrection of extinct species such as the dodo and the Tasmanian tiger—is an area where the essentially secular attitudes of modern society come into sharp conflict with many religious attitudes, principally fundamentalist Christianity of the sort that Schultz preaches to his born-again congregation in the Rose Cathedral. The crisis in Mara's faith in her scientific integrity is prompted by a challenge from an area usually considered irrelevant to the concerns of scientific inquiry: the miraculous tenets of Christianity.

Mara's realisation of the full extent to which she had been duped occurs after she has implanted in Mary-Beth's womb one of the young woman's ova, which, she believes, had been fertilised by genetic material obtained from the sterile Schultz. The first warning comes more by way of a break of trust than anything else. Mary-Beth had pleaded successfully for the first child of her union with Schultz to be a girl, and the preacher-mogul seemed to agree. As she examines images of the embryo within the young woman's womb, Mara notices an anomaly, a protuberance on the foetus which should not be there—not an abnormality, she is quick to realise, but an entirely normal though unwelcome penis.

Then follows the most shocking of her discoveries. Scanlon's fascination with examining the minute particles of organic material adhering to the relics in Grossman's collection, matching them in order to determine whether any two or more come from the same source, was more than a product of his obsession with all manifestations of the DNA. He was searching for remnants of the genuine, historical Christ, in order to replicate his genetic individuality and to place it in an egg extracted from Mary-Beth's ovary, one from which Mary-Beth's own genetic coding had been entirely removed. In short, Mara realises, she has been an unwitting dupe in an attempt to resurrect Christ, and that Mary-Beth's 'conception' was, in its own way, just as 'immaculate' as that of her near-namesake, the

Virgin, who was merely a vessel to carry the divine seed to fruition. Mara's greatest dilemma comes where her secular, materialistic certainties are challenged by the myths of a religion she had discarded in her youth.

In her distress and alarm—though it is not entirely clear to her why she should find this so shocking and alarming, since a matter of religious conviction is not involved here—Mara consults the gospel story of the Annunciation:

> *What was I seeking in these texts? Contradictions? There were more than enough of those. Historical inaccuracies? Proof that He never existed at all—not as the son of God, certainly, but not even as a man, as an actual historical figure?*
> *(p. 247)*

When she upbraids Scanlon, he expresses genuine surprise that she should regard this 'resurrection' as being at all different from his tricks with the dodo or the Tasmanian tiger:

> *Stay cool. She's carrying a clone of someone dead for two thousand years. Jesus Christ? Maybe, but who was he? The bastard son of some Roman legionary.*
> *(pp. 251–2)*

And he deflates her agonised, half-recognised doubts with serene certainty:

> *'Scanlon,' I called after him.*
> *He turned, half-smiling, reassured at the sound of his surname, a sign that I was softening: 'Mmm?'*
> *'What if it is God?'*
> *He laughed, and moved on again: 'We're the gods,' he called back over his shoulder.*

*I had no belief in God, or gods, yet there seemed an enormous
tastelessness in this. His quickness, his restless mind had
drawn me to him months before, and now suddenly freed me
from him. That quickness was merely a kind of decadence, that
restless mind was too easily exhausted, searching always for
new ideas, new sensations, new intellectual thrills.*
(p. 253)

She decides therefore to intervene, in a god-like way
perhaps, by aborting the foetus in Mary-Beth's womb, and
further, she conducts a raid on Scanlon's laboratory,
committing the greatest of scientific crimes, the
destruction of carefully, devotedly assembled research
material.

Mara's outrage at the trick played on her, on Mary-Beth
and perhaps even on science itself, seems to be prompted
by complex considerations in which religious scruples
play no part at all. She is incensed at the way she has been
used and duped, she is distressed by what she sees as the
bad taste of Scanlon's jiggery-pokery, and she experiences
a sense of fellow-feeling with Mary-Beth, as much a dupe
in the affair as herself. Yet *Honk If You Are Jesus* contains
hints, subtly but tellingly placed throughout the novel, to
suggest that Mara's distress and anger are by no means
entirely free of those religious considerations which she
had discarded in favour of a rational, scientific view of
·life.

As she destroys, methodically, ruthlessly, the contents of
Scanlon's laboratory, burning the strips of X-ray film in
order to remove any possibility of his reconstructing
Christ's DNA from the images recorded there, she deviates
from her determination quite curiously when she comes
upon the bits and pieces of organic material Scanlon had
extracted from Grossman's collection of relics.

I jemmied open the fridge using the foot of a nearby tripod. The three phials inside were clearly labelled: Nail of Monza, Armenia IV, Bone Fragment XII. *I smashed the seals of the first two phials and shook out their contents—whitish, translucent pasta-strands of mega-DNA—into a nearby drain. The last phial I gripped tightly for some time, wanting to break this last seal also, but unable to force myself to it. For reasons I could not fully comprehend at the time, I dropped this third phial—The Nail of Monza—into my shoulder bag.*
(pp. 271 2)

It is with this relic, and with one of her own ova, which she had extracted from herself in her infatuation with the high-tech wizardry provided for her, that she flees to Adelaide, also carrying, either Scanlon's child, the fruit of the last flicker of her fertility, or, to follow a teasingly ambiguous possibility implanted in the novel, the material to manufacture another, more exalted, fruit of her womb.

☙

Honk If You Are Jesus is a work of fiction, not an ethical or theological tract. The implications of Mara's outrage at the attempted cloning of Christ, her apparently curious decision not to destroy entirely Scanlon's collection of material, and indeed to appropriate some of it for herself are, therefore, never spelt out clearly. They are 'justified' in terms of her character, in terms of the particular world Goldsworthy creates within the confines of the novel.

  There are, nevertheless, hints that her actions are prompted by scruples not entirely free of religious implications. Throughout the novel, Mara's thoughts turn to religion, or at least to the practices and rituals of

Christianity which, she believes, she has discarded in favour of scientific rationalism. She ascribes this to her upbringing, to the influence of her father, a preacher, and to the conformist, inward-looking priorities of the rural Australia in which she grew up.

Yet she returns, time and time again throughout the novel, to her early experiences, to the way in which religion had surrounded her life. Clearly she has not been able to banish entirely the demands of a system of belief which her scientific, rational self prompts her to see as so much superstition. It has left a residue within her, prompting her—as much as her outrage at the poor taste of Scanlon's sleight-of-hand—to sabotage Schultz's grandiose ambitions.

So she reaches a complex and ambiguous realisation as she flees from the Gold Coast to the stuffy safety of Adelaide, carrying her own holy relics, or the consequences of her sacrilege. As she is suspended between heaven and earth in a floating metal capsule, she recalls a visit she had paid to the cemetery of Père Lachaise in Paris, where many famous and infamous dead are buried. It is a place Goldsworthy had already visited in the poem 'Cimetière Père Lachaise'. The speaker of that poem, like Mara, visits the graves of the famous: Oscar Wilde, Victor Hugo and Jim Morrison. Mara, like the speaker in the poem, marvels at the cult that had collected around Morrison, the dead musician, making his grave into the site of a twentieth-century pilgrimage. Yet the gap of years separating the poem and the novel has produced a significant shift of perspective.

Musing among the graves of the cemetery, the poem's speaker remarks:

> *I have no faith in resurrection, or in anything else right now*
> *except the need of tidiness. I rise and bin my bottle,*
> *and walk away clutching my map of the dead*
> *and my single long-stem rose, bypassing Gertrude and Oscar,*
> *searching somewhere between Chopin's grave*
> *and Proust's, for the Tomb of the Homesick Tourist,*
> *open-doored, perhaps, as if ready to receive.*

The novel expands these images into discursive prose:

> *The Parisian dead are buried beneath small granite phone-*
> *boxes, each grave topped by its own thin, vertical chapel. All*
> *morning I stalked back and forth among the rows with my map*
> *of the famous dead . . . I stumbled upon a group of hippie-types,*
> *smoking lumpen, misshapen cigarettes and swigging from a*
> *shared bottle of wine . . .*
> *The name on the rock at their feet was unfamiliar:* Jim
> Morrison.
> *'Jim lives,' one of the women told me, simply, and handed up*
> *the bottle of wine. Those worshippers were my age, but I passed*
> *the bottle down again, and walked quickly away.*
> *(pp. 284–5)*

Unlike the speaker of the poem, though, Mara is troubled by that encounter, especially as she remembers it from the vantage-point of her flight from the fleshpots of the Gold Coast:

> *It seems a human instinct, a human need: to worship the dead,*
> *yes, but to worship them as resurrected, as* not *dead. I'm*
> *thinking now of odd headlines that sometimes catch the eye:*
> The Body Didn't Look Like Elvis, The Death Certificate
> Was Forged . . .

Someone saw him, Risen, in Galilee. *Is there any difference? I had stopped one resurrection, perhaps the most dangerous, but I saw now that there would be others. Not so much to reclaim lost resources—the priceless brain of a Mozart or an Einstein—as for purposes of worship. To praise the dead, more than to use them. There was a need to believe, not so much in the immortality of certain individuals, as in the promise that the immortality of some held for all. If Elvis can live forever, so surely can I.*
(p. 285)

Goldsworthy's novel offers no resolution, no easy formula either dismissing or confirming Mara's realisation. But it acknowledges, by its subject matter, through this wry history of Mara's disillusionment, accompanied as it is by a sexual awakening, that such uncomfortable elements of life cannot be ignored. In that, Goldsworthy challenges not merely the emphases of his earlier writings, but the tenor of much contemporary Australian writing. Ours is a secular age, at least in the literary sphere. Writers might concern themselves with the irrational or the supernatural, but there has been a general reluctance to consider specific religious issues and preoccupations. *Honk If You Are Jesus* is a stylish, sophisticated vehicle for making such issues and preoccupations available for a secular and sceptical age. Mara's career—from her playful Christmas after-dinner speech recounted at the beginning of the novel, in which she considered the medical aspects of the birth at Bethlehem, to her own 'miraculous' pregnancy—reveals that the mysteries of Christianity, and the doggedly held belief of many societies in resurrection and the prospect of immortality, cannot be ignored, that they will return to haunt even the most pragmatic and scientific of people.

This accounts for the deceptively light, almost casual tone that disappointed several early readers and reviewers of *Honk If You Are Jesus*. Goldsworthy seems to have realised that the introspective intensity of many passages in *Maestro* would have detracted from the novel's ability to balance the secular and the divine, the sceptical and the committed. Uncomfortable and possibly disturbing potentialities needed to be approached obliquely, by way of a seemingly jesting, ironic, modern nativity fable. Consequently, the central character is drained of imagination and of all but a purely scientific curiosity. Through her very dedication to her profession and her disdain for irrelevancies—whether Tad's worship of opera or Mary-Beth's of fashionable clothes— Goldsworthy is able to suggest the essential, indeed spiritual, emptiness of such a life precisely because he is able to represent so convincingly the apparently firm philosophical basis on which that life has been built.

Mara's attitude is essentially sensible and sane. It is vital to Goldsworthy's purposes in this novel that Mara's lack of religious belief be established firmly, with verve, and above all with a strong semblance of justification. Recalling her theological duels with her father, she remembers his reply to her suggestion that God should be impeached for war crimes.

'Don't take the Old Testament too literally,' he told me, mildly. 'The Ten Commandments and the prophecies are all that count.'

I went away and read. And then came back. Fine, I said. What kind of egomaniac would put Himself at the centre of the first three Commandments . . . and relegate Thou Shalt Not Murder to seventh spot? . . .

My father glanced up again from his desk. 'Read the New Testament,' he murmured.

97

> *I went away again, and read some more. God did seem to have*
> *grown up a little in the later Testament. Matured. You couldn't*
> *go past the Sermon on the Mount for a serve of spine-tingling*
> *poetry. But what about the magic tricks? If He was a spoilt brat*
> *in the Old, He was a teenage exhibitionist in the New: turning*
> *water into wine, walking on water, rioting in the Temple.*
> *(pp. 146–7)*

Nevertheless, as *Honk If You Are Jesus* reveals by the time
we reach the end of Mara's adventures on the Gold Coast,
the magic, the hocus-pocus, even God's shocking
megalomania, cannot be dismissed as easily as the
teenage Mara is able to pour scorn on the absurdities and
cruelties of the Bible. Humanity's need for such possibly
primitive instincts may not be particularly ennobling, and
they may lead, indeed, to obscenities like Schultz's grand
design. Yet the obverse, the pragmatic, science-orientated
view of life, is no guarantee of greater ethical probity.
Scanlon's levity as much as Schultz's egomania cause
anguish and suffering for the novel's one true victim, the
insipid Mary-Beth, who is as perplexed and puzzled
about the train of events in which she is trapped as her
precursor must have been when the Archangel Gabriel
came to her with his extraordinary annunciation.

There are, nevertheless, dangers and perils in attending
to the siren song of the numinous, or those insinuations
that insist that the world cannot be understood, or human
life conducted in purely secular terms. Mara is not
seduced, at length, by the mumbo-jumbo and the hocus-
pocus of mysticism or by the easy pieties Schultz preaches
in the Rose Cathedral. Yet she resists falling into the
essential nihilism of Scanlon's attitude; that is, since
nothing is charged with particular value, almost no action

may be deemed out of bounds. Consequently both the novel, in its unemphatic, even lighthearted, treatment of a potentially ponderous topic, and its protagonist manage to strike a balance, so to speak, between extremes, between stifling superstition on the one hand, and arid scepticism on the other.

As a result, *Honk If You Are Jesus* is a buoyant account of a miraculous nativity—Mara's discovery of love, as much as her pregnancy. These two events seem to be placed by Goldsworthy as the central 'spiritual' implications of this fine novel. Love may be treacherous, temporary and prone to disappointment. But in a world that cannot guarantee the essential permanence that Christianity, perhaps spuriously, promises, that may be all there is to be expected. Paltry though Mara's experience of love might have been a couple of sexual bouts with a not very prepossessing individual who has, moreover, an ulterior motive in engaging in the brief liaison—it leads nevertheless to her transformation: not into the certainties of faith, but into the creation of life. Consequently, the novel ends with a preparation for a nativity—whether natural or miraculous—with the words of the gospel spelling out the implications of Mara's journey to an engagement with life:

Is it chemical, this sudden optimism? So my mother would tell me. Contentment goes with the condition, she would claim, smugly.

Contentment goes with an original scientific experiment, I might counter, performed under optimal conditions.

In the next room she is preparing our evening meal: some ancient country folk-broth that even a first-trimester stomach might keep down. She is singing to herself, softly, innocently,

transformed already into the sweetest of grandmothers. Soon
she will seek me out, clucking her tongue at the scribbled
gospel-pages scattered on the floor about me.
   'You must eat, dear. And rest. All this work—and you a
doctor! If you aren't going to think of yourself, think of it.'
   We shall all be changed, in a moment, in the twinkling of an
eye.
(pp. 289–90)

So that whether the new life Mara is bearing in her womb
is another Christ or Scanlon's child is ultimately beside
the point. What matters—and seems to matter intensely—
is committent to the fact. Even if she is to become another
Mother of God, she is entering into that state willingly,
with a full recognition of the implications of what she is
about to do, unlike the unfortunate Mary-Beth, a dupe of
Schultz's megalomania and Scanlon's arrogance.

Chapter Five

What Comes Next?

In the stories and novels written before *Honk If You Are Jesus* a vacancy often seems to stand beyond the lives Goldsworthy's work explores. Both the small suburban dramas of the short stories and the larger catastrophes of *Maestro* end in disappointment, or at least in the characters' being obliged to compromise, to come to terms with lives that offer little hope of fulfilment or satisfaction. There is nothing beyond the humdrum life of the suburbs charted in the three collections of short fiction—no possibility of any lasting achievement and certainly no spiritual comfort. Even the provisional and tentative relationships between men and women—for Goldsworthy's world is almost exclusively heterosexual—end in disappointment, betrayal or the death of love. There is no scope for heroism, precious little for altruism or idealism; the predominant tone of Goldsworthy's earlier work, therefore, is essentially ironic, quick to discover shams and pretentiousness, but unable to entertain anything more lasting or consoling.

In that aspect of his work Goldsworthy may have been mirroring the predominant lack of spirituality in contemporary Australian life. His stories pitch themselves within the secular world where Australians of the past fifty years or so have attempted to discover their social and cultural priorities. It is a world, by and large, which shuns those larger questions that philosophy and religion usually contemplate. The meaning of life is not questioned in these explorations of the suburban mentality because there seems little point to it: life ultimately appears to have little meaning. Even loyalty, trust or altruism are as likely as not to be compromised. As for death, that is largely overlooked, perhaps because it is nothing other than an inescapable biological fact.

Maestro reveals, however, a tentative and provisional engagement with issues which Goldsworthy's earlier writing, and also the Australia it chronicles, had generally ignored. Albeit obliquely, the novel considers one of the most horrible outrages of the century, the systematic extermination of Europeans of Jewish descent during the thirties and forties, and it addresses itself to the conundrum George Steiner posed in *In Bluebeard's Castle*: how could the Germans, those people renowned for their respect for art and culture, condone such uncivilised barbarism?

Such questions are alien to the emphases of much Australian writing, except perhaps where the plight of Aborigines is considered. Otherwise the material on which Australian writers are obliged to work, and also the horizons of the culture within which they are obliged to exist—no matter with how many misgivings—do not allow much scope for such concerns. Goldsworthy's stratagem in *Maestro* is identical to that employed by several earlier writers, notably Patrick White in *The Eye of the Storm*. That stratagem or device is twofold. In the first instance an alien, disturbing individual, a survivor of that great obscenity, is introduced into a more or less humdrum world, whether that of a patrician mansion in Sydney or the steamy Darwin of the sixties. In the second place, the terrible experiences those people endured in the death camps and cattle-trucks, which have maimed them or else rendered them grotesque, are approached obliquely—in *Maestro* through Paul's peeling away the onion-skins of the enigma of Eduard Keller.

The sense is inescapable that Australian writers experience some difficulty in dealing with massive brutality, and therefore with that particular kind of heroism that does not manifest itself in a type of Voss-like hubris, but rather in self-sacrifice, as in the essentially unheroic heroism of Keller, who had voluntarily condemned himself to the death camps. It seems equally clear, however, that many of them, including Goldsworthy, are troubled by that difficulty, or, to put it another way, that they are dissatisfied by the limited scope the society they must reflect in their writings offers for the contemplation of the larger questions of existence, and of the manifestations of good and evil that emerge in such circumstances. To consider those topics is, in a way, to endow a story or a novel with an essentially spiritual dimension. It is towards such a dimension that Goldsworthy's later work makes some tentative steps.

Honk If You Are Jesus, for all its ironic comedy, the good fun it has with the vanities and hypocrisies of the theological theme park into which Mara strays, does nevertheless address itself to issues that lie outside the confirmed secularism of people such as Scanlon, or of Mara herself, despite her early training in theological disputation. It forces consideration of questions that lie, in part at least, beyond ethics, and encroach on essentially theological questions. The novel's consideration of these issues and possibilities is by no means direct or unconditional— much of its strength is derived from the substantial conflict between the secular and the spiritual, as Goldsworthy, by way of Mara's adventures, tries to reconcile a scientific scepticism with the recognition of the human need for spirituality, even though that need, more often than not, manifests itself in dubious myths and mysteries.

The myths and mysteries must, still, be considered, and once considered their effect on the shape and tendency of Goldsworthy's work is remarkable. *Honk If You Are Jesus* offers at its end a resolution of sorts: there is a promise of at least temporary and limited contentment as Mara celebrates her own, even if dubious, fertility, anticipating the coming of the child she is carrying, while considering the implication of those once-familiar Bible texts that promise redemption and immortality. While not subscribing to any metaphysic, *Honk If You Are Jesus* is able at least to celebrate biological immortality, the continuation of the species, the peopling of the earth, possibilities usually regarded with deep misgivings by the secular scepticism or nihilism that dominates the culture of the late twentieth century.

Goldsworthy's most recently published work, *Little Deaths*, a collection of shorter fiction, takes that concern a step further, especially in 'Jesus Wants Me For A Sunbeam', a powerful and disturbing novella. The other stories in the collection seem to look backwards: they explore a world similar to that charted in his earlier short stories—though several of them represent an oblique engagement with issues of the sort that arise in *Maestro* and *Honk If You Are Jesus*, issues that endow 'Jesus Wants Me For A Sunbeam' with its sombre effect. The stories deal with varieties of death: literal, metaphoric, social. Each of them is, in a way, only a little death because nothing, no possibility or hope, seems to exist beyond it. And for that reason, of course, those little deaths have depressingly large implications.

In 'The Car Keys', Barbara, a married woman, has to deal with the embarrassment of explaining what a middle-aged man seized by a fatal heart attack was doing in her bedroom. The opening words reveal the extent to which Goldsworthy's short fiction retains its concerns within tightly contained structures:

> *Later, Barbara remembered a platitude she had read somewhere: an orgasm was a kind of death, a little death.*
>
> *A death*-throe.
>
> *(p. 2)*

At the end of the story she guiltily removes evidence of the way in which her own little death led to her lover's 'great' death by stealing his car keys from the hospital where he has died.

In 'Pointing the Bone', Philip, an angry bereaved husband, berates his friends who, according to him, spread a malicious rumour of his wife's seemingly non-existent cancer, blaming them for the cancer which killed her shortly afterwards. His burst of passion—

> *He shook himself free: 'No—I won't calm down. I can't forgive you. You willed her into the grave—all of you. You willed her to have cancer. You . . . voted for it. It was like—like she was elected, or something. An election by gossip . . .'*
>
> *(p. 51)*

—is followed by exhaustion and, for his friends, by embarrassment and shame. But the story stops short of addressing what the major work in *Little Deaths*, the novella 'Jesus Wants Me For A Sunbeam' considers fully; the impact of such a death not merely on the lives but on the way-of-life, so to speak, of the bereaved. This story, as in the other short pieces in the collection, displays the caution, or even perhaps anxiety, in Goldsworthy's short fiction which makes him pull back from considering the full, sometimes appalling implications of the worlds he depicts.

No doubt significantly, in some of the stories included in the collection, 'little deaths' end in survival, yet they signal nevertheless an ending. In 'The Nice Surprise' a troublesome grandmother is removed from her grand-child when his parents pretend that she has died, so that she is obliged at length to think of herself as dead. 'The Death of Daffy Duck' relates how a man who saves the life of a friend choking on a piece of food finds himself shunned as a friendship comes to die. A chemistry teacher, whose methods and knowledge have remained stagnant for decades, faces the emptiness of the end of her career in 'Tea and Macaroons'.

It is only in the novella, though ambiguously and tenta-tively, that Goldsworthy explores the full implications of dying in a way that goes somewhat beyond the finality of death, or of the little deaths of the kind that may culminate in a survival of sorts.

There is not, any more than there is in *Honk If You Are Jesus*, an insistence on an afterlife, on the miraculous tenets of Christianity. But there is a disturbing, though significant, sense that death is somehow endowed with meaning—just as for Mara the resurrection of Christ's genetic material is not entirely justifiable in purely secular scientific terms. And, most importantly perhaps, death may become a positive act of affirmation.

'Jesus Wants Me For A Sunbeam', for all its brevity and concision, represents a notable development in Goldsworthy's writing. In a mere forty-seven pages he addresses issues which, from one point of view, he had been circling around, avoiding yet not coming into contact with, in much of his earlier work. Those issues, moreover, involve a consideration of the meaning of life, and therefore of death. It is a bold, disturbing examination of questions often shunned in contemporary writing. Yet, paradoxically but significantly, Goldsworthy compresses material that could have—perhaps should have—sustained a full-length novel. In that brevity some of the anxiety that characterises much of his writing (and not merely the decision to collaborate with Matthews on *Magpie*) may be glimpsed.

∽

Rick and Linda represent all that is sane, healthy and attractive in the idealism of the kind displayed by many of the characters in Goldsworthy's earlier collections of short fiction—an idealism compromised more often than not by weakness and by the misleading allure of a consumers' world. They seem to have avoided the traps and pitfalls of the modern world: their marriage is happy, harmonious, and they are blessed with two charming children:

'One of each,' friends remarked, enviously, after the birth of their second. 'You're so lucky.'

> Linda feigned chagrin at this: 'Credit where credit's due,
> please—it took years of careful planning.'
> She was not entirely joking. If their good fortune was not
> exactly planned, it was, she felt, at least deserved. It was
> earned.
> (p. 90)

Their harmonious life is a product of like tastes, like principles—an informed, humane and socially responsible acceptance of the priorities of middle-class life, tempered by a sane recognition of changing values and responsibilities:

> They married in St Paul's, Linda's parish church. They chose the
> recently arrived Reverend Cummings as celebrant—a young
> student-priest, or priest-intern, whom Linda had met through
> the church youth group—rather than the older rector that her
> parents preferred. Bill Cummings was their own age; he
> permitted a revised modern set of vows in which both partners
> promised to love, honour and cherish, but from which the
> ancient asymmetrical duty of wifely obedience had been deleted.
> (pp. 91–2)

So united are they in their love and so secure is the manner in which this young couple grows and matures together, that they seem to merge into one—each takes on the physical characteristics of the other:

> Their physical resemblance to each other, near-identical height
> and body-build, seemed to become more pronounced through
> those first years of marriage, as if eating the same food and
> sharing the same exercise caused an even closer convergence of
> body-types. Without exactly planning it, Rick permitted his

hair to grow a little longer, Linda cropped hers shorter; they
chose, independently, similar gold-rimmed glasses. They often
wore each other's T-shirts, and even, at a stretch, before the
birth of Ben, each other's jeans.
(p. 93)

Such self-sufficiency, Rick and Linda find, needs to be nurtured and protected. Aware of the suffering and deprivation in so much of the world, they try to share their good fortune by donating generously to charity, by fostering a child through World Care. Their ambitions are altruistic, by no means self-indulgent. When they receive photographs of their foster-child, or later a series of 'identically flat and formulaic' letters:

They decided not to answer these letters. It seemed demeaning,
even humiliating, to compel a child to write thank you letters,
to report annually to its benefactors—to beg, in essence. It
seemed best to keep at some sort of distance.
(p. 96)

Their reluctance to acknowledge those pathetic, no doubt contrived, letters probably stems, however, from a different fear. Linda becomes sensitive to violence, to the painful and disturbing elements of life. After the birth of their second child, Emma, she decides to stop going to the movies—too much glorying in violence and sadism. Television is next to be discarded:

The lead story on the news was surely no more horrific
or blood-spattered than usual, but Linda shivered—suddenly,
involuntarily—and averted her eyes from the screen.
(p. 97)

When she insists that they turn the set off, Rick offers mild resistance:

> *'Why do they show things like that?'* . . .
> *'Perhaps we should try to understand it.'*
> *'How can you understand it? A man who murders his entire family, then himself!'*
> *She shuddered again, as disturbed by her own blunt summary of events as she had been by the original story.*
> *'Maybe he did it out of love,' Rick suggested, weirdly.*
> *She stared at him, incredulous:* 'What?'
> *He watched the blank screen, as if waiting for more information, trying to understand this odd germ of a thought, to grow it.*
> *'Misplaced love,' he said, groping. 'If you're depressed, and the world is not worth living in, you want to save your loved ones from it. You want to protect them.'*
> *(pp. 97–8)*

Linda is horrified, and Rick too finds himself shocked by this worrying alien thought, so contrary to the serene confidence of their life. But, as the rest of the novella displays, it identifies the way in which those certainties and that confidence are revealed to be little more than complacency.

And so they come gradually to withdraw into themselves, into the perfection of their family, discarding the mean and ugly vulgarity of the world. When the intrusive television set, with its lurid images of horror and brutality, is banished, they find all the diversion they need in reading aloud to each other from cherished books:

> *an intellectual dowry of children's books, old school texts, gift-sets of Shakespeare and Shaw and Jane Austen and assorted*

Brontës, plus, from Linda's side, everything that Dickens had ever written: a metre length, at least, of matching volumes, bound in calf, plus assorted school paperback versions of the same titles.
(p. 100)

These timeless classics prove sufficient for their needs; there is no occasion to buy new books—that would be to open themselves to fresh, possibly disturbing, influences—for here, in these safely familiar books, is all that they could desire.

Isolated from the wider world, their small, shared life contracted even more tightly about their children, their board-games and book-readings. Old friends from University, staff-room colleagues from school—many still single—were rarely seen. There seemed so little time.
(pp. 101–2)

In that perfection, within the protection of love, their self sufficiency comes to be tested by a visitation of the seemingly irrational or even perhaps the malevolent.

❧

Emma, the daughter, contracts a seemingly trivial virus, picked up at her play-group, no doubt; a sore throat and no more than that. It proves to be, however, the first symptom of leukemia: Rick and Linda are obliged to learn how to deal with the unthinkable—the prospect that a healthy child is destined to die from a terrible ailment, the course of which might be temporarily slowed but not arrested. The bulk of the novella contains a restrained, chillingly direct but deeply moving account of the way in which Linda and Rick are dragged out of the protective enclosure they had built around their lives to come face to face with that appallingly inevitable fact.

Goldsworthy captures the oscillations of hope and despair as the impersonal procedures of diagnosis proceed to their conclusion—the child has, at best, three years of life remaining:

> *Three years was the length of her life to date: she was being*
> *offered her entire lifetime, repeated. Her parents sat watching*
> *her, breathing a little more easily. For the moment they could*
> *fall no further; they could even permit themselves a small*
> *ration of hope. A cure might well be found in three years. A*
> *marrow donor might even be found, although Eve [the*
> *specialist physician] was as frank as always on this: odd blood-*
> *lines in Rick's family—a Finnish great-grandparent—had left*
> *the child with a rare tissue-type, possibly unique.*
> *(p. 105)*

They find, moreover, that as the disease runs its course, and as their emotional and physical resources are tried and assaulted, they are no longer able to welcome, as they had during the early days, their physician's blunt, uncompromising honesty:

> *Their need for bluntness had passed; they now wanted*
> *cosmetics. Despite Eve's advice, they had also come to depend*
> *on worry. Worrying was far from useless, they sensed: the*
> *worry process was a restless working-through of possibilities*
> *and permutations, an exhaustive examination of every path,*
> *every fork in the path.*
> *(p. 109)*

That restlessness leads in turn to an immersion in activities—membership of the Make-a-Wish Foundation and leukemia support groups—which provide a channel for the energies unlocked by anxiety and despair.

Next follows guilt, and beyond guilt a search for scapegoats:

When the search for paths into the future ended in blind alleys, there was still the past to examine. The feeling was inescapable that they were somehow to blame, that it might even help if they were to blame. Had Linda taken some harmful drug during pregnancy? Drunk one glass too many of wine? Had there been something else in Emma's childhood environment? Something chemical or unnatural? Some toxin? If they could not blame themselves they blamed others. Linda's father—a heavy smoker, two packs a day—came under suspicion briefly.
(p. 111)

At length Linda and Rick must acknowledge their impotence. There is no explanation for Emma's disease, nothing to blame, nothing to hope for. Neither the fact that the three-year milestone had been passed nor an appeal to the supernatural is capable of offering any resistance to its progress:

Neither the protective magic of such gestures, nor the prayers offered up in church, could ward off the greater power of statistics, and the laws of probability. The disease returned a few months later; 'active treatment' was stopped shortly afterwards, after a last failure of response to chemotherapy. The phrase, and its coy replacement—'palliative treatment'— seemed out-of-character for Eve Harrison: an evasion, which in itself told the parents of the seriousness of Emma's plight.
(p. 114)

And so they must face the reality of their situation, forcing them also to recognise the consequences of their self-absorption, or at least their concentration on Emma, through its effects on Ben, the by-now largely neglected other child.

❧

Up to this point, 'Jesus Wants Me For A Sunbeam' is a dispassionate but by no means unfeeling exploration of a moral and social dilemma for which the child's terrible disease becomes an effective focus. Goldsworthy's control and ability to manipulate tone and nuance are both admirable. From the opening measures of the story, where Rick and Linda's serenely responsible life is described, a sense of unease, even perhaps of foreboding, is deftly introduced. It is not so much a matter of our being made to feel that they are too fortunate, that their life is proceeding too smoothly along well-planned paths, as the suspicion that their essentially sane and civilised attempt to conduct their lives along commendably responsible lines is unwittingly forcing them to retreat behind walls of fantasy and wish-fulfilment.

As they withdraw more and more into cosy perfection—discarding anything unpleasant, anything that seems to them contrary to the values they cherish—they are effectively isolating themselves from life, preferring to dwell within the essential unreality of their little world. The cinema, television with its lurid images of carnage and brutality, even books other than their well-loved classics all seem to acknowledge the world as it is, rather than as Rick and Linda would wish it to be. Responsibility and sanity ultimately lead, therefore, to irresponsibility and a dangerous escapism.

The cool control of tone and marshalling of the devices of a novella—which must compress, abstract and epitomise—allow Goldsworthy to insinuate such possibilities without the necessity to stress or to state them. Technically, the novella represents a considerable mastery of form and narrative procedures. That essential obliqueness also allows certain other implications to arise which come to dominate the tale's striking climax. It is there that Goldsworthy's tactful, provisional and tentative exploration of the religious implications of the worlds he depicts—a tendency already evident in *Honk If You Are Jesus*—comes into focus

In their withdrawal from the world Rick and Linda have also abandoned the habit of church-going, which had been in any event more a matter of social form and ritual than the result of deep conviction. Because they are representatives of a phenomenon Goldsworthy had examined in his earlier fiction—urban, professional people who grew up in a world becoming rapidly secularised—they attempt to organise their lives on secular and rational lines In a way that differs from Mara's in incidentals only, the supernatural, whether divine or infernal, benevolent or malicious, fails to enter into their scheme of things. Yet when it becomes clear to them that reason is able to offer neither an explanation of why their child should have been singled out nor a guide for easing their anguish or the child's suffering, they make a few, tentative steps towards the metaphysical:

As the end also became clearer to Rick and Linda, they resumed church-going, choosing to look pity in the eye, to stare it down, to spurn it. In part this return to the fold was still a search for the routines of normality, an attempt to travel backwards in time; in part it was a last desperate reaching out—not for

miracles, perhaps, but at least for answers.
(pp. 118–9)

Nevertheless, when answers of a sort are provided, by the Reverend Cummings, who had obligingly altered the form of the marriage ceremony for them, they are incapable of accepting or dealing with the kinds of answers he provides:

'Don't forget the power of faith,' he exhorted over innumerable
cups of tea. 'The power of prayer.'
Linda had reached exasperation point.
'I don't understand,' she said, 'why that would help. And if
it did, what kind of God would insist on it? Why should we
have to beg for favours?' . . .
'I don't want to sound glib,' he murmured, 'but if we knew
all the answers—if knowledge was given to us on a plate—
what would be the point of faith?'
(p. 119)

The priest's answers are unsatisfactory, evasive. The little girl's illness is perhaps a test of their faith, he suggests to Linda; perhaps it is harder for her parents than for her. When Linda turns on him with anguish and malice, he finds himself nonplussed and falls back on a comfortable cliché:

He paused before answering, shocked by her harshness. He
licked his lips, his mouth opened and closed without speaking,
groping for an answer that was not quite ready. He was out of
his depth. His avuncular manner had vanished, his eyes
reddened, he was close to tears.
'Remember the story of Abraham and Isaac.' he finally said,
huskily. 'The Lord tested Abraham's faith by asking him to
sacrifice his son?'

> *Despite his anguish, Linda's face instantly purpled with rage.*
> *'Fuck you,' she said. 'And fuck any God who would play*
> *such horrible games.'*
> *(p. 120)*

That is unanswerable. Conventional religion, or at least its
custodian, is no more able here than in *Honk If You Are
Jesus* to resolve the dilemma that torments Linda and
perplexes Mara. Linda's descent into coarse vulgarity is a
measure of her despair, and also a searing recognition that
neither the consolations of religion nor her previously
sane and civilised way of life is capable of teaching her
how to deal with or to accept the unspeakable. Yet
ultimately Linda and Rick—just as in her own way Mara
does—come to an accommodation with the religious, if
not exactly with religion, when faced with the
inevitability of Emma's death.

When the child's rapidly deteriorating condition forces
them to consider not only the fact but also the
consequences of her death, a hitherto unsuspected
possibility arises.

> *Rick first spoke the unspeakable. They lay talking in bed in the*
> *small hours, trying, as always, to talk each other to sleep, to*
> *talk themselves empty, to talk out the day's accumulated*
> *worries.*
> *'Maybe we should all go together,' he said, inserting the*
> *words suddenly, without warning, into a lull in a conversation*
> *about household finances.*
> *'What do you mean?'*
> *'Just that. We shouldn't let her go . . . alone.'*
> *(p. 122)*

The suggestion is 'too crazy', Linda says, even though she

admits that the thought had occurred to her (p. 122). Yet the thought once implanted is almost impossible to banish. Rick, who had upset and shocked Linda with his remarks about the man who had murdered his family and then killed himself, is the first to mention this possibility, but Linda too becomes preoccupied with it. Though the implication is not stated, both now clearly do not see Emma's death as an ending, a finality. There would otherwise be no point to Linda's remark:

> I can't bear to think of her going away—alone. It's as though
> we've cast her out into the woods. Abandoned her, like
> something in a fairy tale. And we won't go with her.
> (p. 123)

These reactions are not, of course, logical or coolly considered; they are the reactions of two distressed, exhausted people. Nevertheless, the notion that one, both, perhaps all three, should accompany Emma seizes hold of them, and for the first time in a relationship which had begun in such harmony and amity, there is rivalry and dissension.

Linda and Rick vie with each other about which of the two should 'go with' Emma, since they soon realise that they cannot subject Ben to the death each seems willing to endure. So they decide, with much whispered disputation and even flashes of anger, that Rick should be the one. When the child is told about their decision, Rick is forced to consider in precise terms the implications both he and Linda had been largely avoiding:

> He realised that she took it for granted that he would choose to
> die with her; it was a wonderful comfort, yes, but his intended

sacrifice—a sacrifice of everything—meant nothing else to her. He saw no selfishness in her reaction, not even the normal self-centredness of a child, but an entirely reasonable interpretation of events to an intelligent six-year old mind. if heaven was such a wonderful place, why wouldn't he choose to come with her?

His own view of the road ahead was a little more terrifying. And yet—at the same time, once the decision had been made and was locked in place—oddly exciting. A far, far better place? He doubted it. Whatever faith he had once had now seemed shallow: a routine, social faith. He felt he was going nowhere, just ending—but perhaps those last few days, and especially nights, of peace, would make it worthwhile. And perhaps, just perhaps . . .
(p. 130)

The novella offers no certainties. It does not, cannot resolve the question posed by that *'perhaps'*, just as it retains the depressing possibility that all faith is perhaps nothing other than a 'routine, social faith'. Moreover, even entertaining the possibility that there is something after death—if only to make the last days of Emma's life a little less terrifying for her—could be seen to create even greater suffering, and a great injustice to Ben, the child who would be left behind, without father, without sister:

The boy stared at him, uncomprehending—perhaps, even at nine, disbelieving. Explanations that had sounded profound the night before—talk of journeys, of waking in heaven, of future meetings—now sounded banal, or untrue, or even meaningless. Not for the first time, panic overwhelmed Rick, a wave of terror of the enormity, and absurdity, of the scheme.
(pp. 131–2)

Nevertheless, even though assurance cannot be obtained, even though Rick is aware of the harm, damage or worse he is about to do to his son, the 'Plan' is pursued. The family spends one or two days in an imitation of normal family life—games of monopoly, visits to a Pizza Hut— then father and daughter die.

❧

'Jesus Wants Me For A Sunbeam', because of its structural clarity and through Goldsworthy's fine control of tone, avoiding both the maudlin and the sensational, represents his most accomplished achievement up to this time. Within its modest scope—a remarkable feat of distillation, indeed—it also signals a focusing of issues that have come gradually to preoccupy his writing. The novella's resonances, its dispassionate but also anxiety-filled examination of issues often ignored by the largely secular temper of contemporary life, highlight problems and worrying possibilities which characters like Paul, in his search for Keller's 'secret', and Mara, in her brush with religious obsession, also encounter.

Rick and Linda travel a similar road. They too start life, as the characters of Goldsworthy's short stories commonly do, within the materialistic pieties of contemporary Australia. But unlike those earlier characters they are forced to consider death in a way that they had not been obliged to do—unless they were exceptional, 'foreign', and to some extent eccentric, like Eduard Keller. Rick and Linda have to choose, and they must also participate, in a way, in death, each accepting a different path, a different means of coming to terms with it, or at least of acknowledging its presence, its inescapability.

That is an essentially religious attitude. Neither of them

considers those questions which *Honk If You Are Jesus*, by way of its genetic conceits, plays with and then mocks—that the individual may die but immortality continues through the species or by means of clever tinkering such as Scanlon's. Rick and Linda are forced to do what their religion had taught them to do—even if they had not heeded its stern precept—that death must become an essential 'fact of life'.

Clearly, neither here nor elsewhere in his more recent writing is Goldsworthy a religious or doctrinal apologist. The banal pieties of conventional Christianity are made to seem as irrelevant in 'Jesus Wants Me For A Sunbeam' as they are in *Honk If You Are Jesus*. Bringing the notion of death into one's view of life, the story suggests, may, indeed, be destructive, cruel and selfish. One of the strengths of the novella is that it does not overlook the possibility that, for all his high-minded talk of sacrifice, Rick is merely looking for an escape from the intolerable, that his inability to face the prospect of their life after Emma's death is a sign of irresponsibility and self-absorption. Yet the other possibility—that 'perhaps'—will not be banished. At the end of this novella there is, in a way unprecedented among Goldsworthy's earlier writings, a sense of an essential mystery, that something may follow after life, that the secular pieties and certainties of that section of Australian life which he had chronicled with devotion in his earlier work may not represent all that needs be said about life and also about death.

'Jesus Wants Me For A Sunbeam' is poised, therefore, between those two antithetical possibilities. Does it represent, within its restrained, perhaps deliberately confined scope, an intimation of what will come next? Since Goldsworthy is still relatively young, since he no

doubt has many productive years before him, to reach
conclusions would be inappropriate. Instead we should
attend perhaps to 'What Comes Next?', Goldsworthy's
own prophesy, in a way, which is contained in a poem
appended as an *envoi* to *Little Deaths*.

There is nothing as empty as the future,
or as bleached and pale blue: a type of summer,
a long school-holiday, unpunctuated even
by our little lives, rounded with brackets.

Outside those brackets, what? Or—far worse—why?
Don't ask so many questions, wise adults
repeated, often, when I was young—
but each year I push an extra candle

through the crust and panic:
another pilot-flame to extinguish, quickly,
lest something uncontrollable ignites,
or I find myself breaking through icing

into the molten stuff beneath, suddenly
reduced to composite materials.
Perhaps this is the final homecoming:
a fair and even redistribution of matter;

my atoms permitted to cease their restless
jiggling, at peace among the other particles;
my bits and pieces returned to where
I sprang from—or less I, than me;

and less me, than him: his handful of carbon
returned to that topsoil, his water-quota—fifty litres—
to those streams and clouds, his ash to that ash;
his dust to that dust, there, no longer mine.

About the Author

Andrew Riemer is a well known critic, academic and writer. He was born in Budapest in 1936. In 1947 his parents settled in Sydney, where he now lives with his wife and two sons. The experiences of his early years in Australia form the basis of his award-winning memoir *Inside Outside*. *Habsburg Café* describes his experiences upon revisiting Eastern Europe. He has also written several books on Shakespeare and is a regular contributor of book reviews to *The Sydney Morning Herald* and *The Age* in Melbourne.

DATE DUE

10.11.94		
30.11.94		
2 2 AUG 1995		
23 Oct, 95		
25.10.95		
3.11.95		
8 11.95		
13.11.95		
20. AUG. 1996		
16 Nov, 96		
28. NOV 1997		